All Shall Be Well

A MODERN-LANGUAGE VERSION OF THE
REVELATION OF JULIAN OF NORWICH

All Shall Be Well

A MODERN-LANGUAGE VERSION OF THE
REVELATION OF JULIAN OF NORWICH

ELLYN SANNA

All Shall Be Well: A MODERN-LANGUAGE VERSION OF THE REVELATION OF JULIAN OF NORWICH

Copyright © 2018 by Anamchara Books, a Division of Harding House Publishing Service, Inc. All rights reserved. No part of this publication may be reproduced or transmitted in any form or by any means, electronic or mechanical, including photocopying, recording, taping, or any information storage and retrieval system, without permission from the publisher.

Anamchara Books
Vestal, New York 13850
WWW.ANAMCHARABOOKS.COM

IngramSpark 2020 paperback ISBN: 978-1-62524-789-6

Library of Congress Control Number 2010943022

Author: Ellyn Sanna
Hazelnut symbols by Kirill Smalugov, Dreamstime.
Printed in the United States of America.

Scripture quotations labeled NIV are taken from the HOLY BIBLE, NEW INTERNATIONAL VERSION®, copyright 1973, 1978, 1984 Biblica. Used by permission of Zondervan. All rights reserved. Scripture quotations labeled NKJV are from the New King James Version, copyright © 1982 by Thomas Nelson, Inc. Used by permission. All rights reserved. Scripture quotations marked NLT are taken from the Holy Bible, New Living Translation, copyright 1996, 2004. Used by permission of Tyndale House Publishers, Inc., Wheaton, Illinois 60189. All rights reserved. Scripture quotations labeled YLT are from Young's Literal Translation, which was written by Robert Young in 1898 and is in the public domain.

Table of Contents

Introduction 9
I. A Revelation of Love in Sixteen Showings 19
II. Three Gifts from God 23
III. Suffering with Christ 26
The First Revelation 29
IV. Christ's Endurance and My Heart's Joy 31
V. The Hazelnut 34
VI. Our Highest and Deepest Prayer 38
VII. The Revelation of Faith 42
VIII. Sharing in Love 45
IX. God Is Everything That Is Good 47
The Second Revelation 51
X. Seeking Versus Seeing 53
The Third Revelation 57
XI. The Midpoint 59
The Fourth Revelation 63
XII. Christ's Blood Is Love's Bounty 65
The Fifth Revelation 67
XIII. Christ's Death Overcomes the Enemy 69
The Sixth Revelation 73
XIV. Our Affirmation in Heaven 75
The Seventh Revelation 77
XV. Fleeting Sorrow, Constant Peace 79
The Eighth Revelation 83
XVI. A Portion of Christ's Endurance 85
XVII. Ultimate Pain 87
XVIII. His Pain Is Ours 91
XIX. Jesus Is My Heaven 93

XX. In Love, Christ Bore Each of Our Sorrows 96
XXI. Temporary Pain Yields Endless Knowledge 99
The Ninth Revelation 101
XXII. Love That Is Greater Than All Pain 103
XXIII. The Glad Giver 106
The Tenth Revelation 109
XXIV. The Wounds of Love 111
The Eleventh Revelation 113
XXV. In Mary, We Know We Are Loved 115
The Twelfth Revelation 117
XXVI. "It Is I" 119
The Thirteenth Revelation 121
XXVII. All Shall Be Well 123
XXVIII. Christ Lives in Our Love for Each Other 126
XXIX. Sin's Harm 128
XXX. Truth Revealed, Truth Hidden 129
XXXI. Christ Thirsts for Our Well-Being 131
XXXII. The Great Deed That Heals All Deeds 134
XXXIII. Blind Faith Balanced with Mental Focus 137
XXXIV. God Reveals All We Need to Know 139
XXXV. Particular Attachments Hinder Us 141
XXXVI. Our Sin Does Not Hinder God's Goodness 145
XXXVII. The Desire for Wholeness Lives in All Souls 148
XXXVIII. The Mark of Sin Is Turned into a Mark of
    Worth 150
XXXIX. Our Bruises Bring Us to God 153
XL. Safe Even in Sin 155
The Fourteenth Revelation 159
XLI. All You Ask Is Grounded in Me 161
XLII. Prayer Is a Taste of Heaven 165
XLIII. Prayer Unites Our Souls with God 169
More Thoughts on the Fourteen Revelations 173
XLIV. The Human Soul Reflects the Divine 175

TABLE OF CONTENTS

XLV. Our Nature-Substance and Our Sense-Souls 177
XLVI. A Paradox 180
XLVII. We Become Misaligned When We Become Self-Centered 183
XLVIII. Mercy and Grace Are Love's Two Faces 186
XLIX. Union with God Gives Peace 189
L. Bringing Our Questions to God 192
LI. Double Vision 194
LII. We Have Reason to Mourn—and Reason for Joy 206
LIII. Endless Love 211
LIV. Faith Is Merely This: Believing We Are in God and God Is in Us 214
LV. Christ Erases Humanity's Double Death 216
LVI. Our Sensual Nature and Our Spiritual Essence Are United 220
LVII. Our Two Natures Are One in Christ 224
LVIII. Nature, Mercy, Grace 227
LIX. Christ Is the True Mother 231
LX. The Loving Mother 234
LXI. Divine Love Can Never Be Broken 237
LXII. Always Safe 240
LXIII. Sin Is Unnatural 242
The Fifteenth Revelation 247
LXIV. You Shall Go Higher 249
LXV. No Need to Worry 253
LXVI. The End of the Showings 256
The Sixteenth Revelation 259
LXVII. Jesus Makes His Home in Our Souls 261
LXVIII. Overcoming Troubles 265
LXIX. Saved from the Enemy 267
LXX. We Rely on Faith 269
LXXI. Our Protector's Face 272
LXXII. Meddling with Sin Clouds Our Vision 274

LXXIII. Soul Sickness Comes in Two Forms 279
LXXIV. No Fear Pleases God Except the Awe of God 283
LXXV. Awe Is Heaven's Courtesy 287
LXXVI. Separation from God Is the Only Hell 289
LXXVII. Don't Blame Yourself! 292
LXXVIII. Even as We Are Lifted Up, Yet We Are
    Humbled 295
LXXIX. Examine Your Own Sin—But No One Else's 297
LXXX. God Is Both Highest and Lowest 299
LXXXI. God Sees Our Lives as Penance 302
LXXXII. In Both Our Rising and Our Falling We Are
    Kept Whole in Love 304
LXXXIII. Life, Love, and Light 307
LXXXIV. Love 309
LXXXV. All Is as It Is: It Is Well 311
LXXXVI. Love Was What It All Meant 312

Introduction

The woman known today only as Julian of Norwich was born in late 1342, and she died around 1412. During these decades of the Middle Ages, the Plague swept through England three times. Some scholars suggest that Julian may have outlived a husband and children, and as I worked on her book, I came to believe that the images she uses in her book indicate she understood motherhood firsthand. Many scholars disagree, however; biographies of her life often indicate that she was a nun who entered a convent at a very early age. Either way, we can only speculate, for we have few confirmed historical details of her life. Certainly, by the time she was a young woman, she had seen many in her community succumb to the Black Death. Survivor guilt may have been what drove her to pray for suffering and sickness.

At any rate, in May 1373, when Julian was thirty-one, she became sick enough that a priest was called to administer the last rites. While she lay on what she thought was her deathbed, she had a series of intense mystical revelations. She called them "showings."

Shortly after this experience, she recovered from her illness. At some point in her life, she became an anchoress, committed to a life of prayer and meditation while confined to a cell adjoining a church.

The Life of an Anchoress

Anchoresses—women who chose to be imprisoned for God—were an accepted part of medieval life, serving a function rather like a counselor or psychologist might today. Although they had chosen a living burial, dying to the world in a very practical way, these women continued to be active in their communities. Nobility and commoners, rich and poor, would have come to Julian's window, seeking her advice and guidance.

An anchoress's life was governed by a "rule," a written structure that prevented excess and abuse. Julian would have probably followed the Ancrene Rule, written early in the thirteenth century, which provided detailed instructions for an anchoress's life. As a result, she would have worn plain clothes and eaten simple meals while living in a small suite of rooms. She would have eaten twice a day between Easter and Holy Cross Day (September 14), and the rest of the year, she would have had only one meal each day. Her anchorage would have had three windows: one that looked into the church, through which she could listen to mass and receive communion; a second that opened into the outside world, allowing people to speak with her and hear her counsel; and a third that looked into an adjoining room, where a servant lived. Unlike Julian, the servant could come and go, entering Julian's suite to bring food and do the cooking and cleaning, so that Julian's time could be devoted completely to prayer and spiritual counsel.

INTRODUCTION

Julian's World

Julian's era was one of turmoil and crisis. Contemporary reports indicate that at least half the population of Norwich died from the Plague; the clergy and undertakers could not keep up with the dead bodies. Meanwhile, other diseases killed the cattle, and harvests failed. In 1381, when Julian was thirty-nine, people became so desperate they rose up in a revolt, looting the churches and monasteries.

During Julian's lifetime, John Wyclif was also preaching against the corruption within the Church; his translation of the Bible into the common language of English brought down on him papal accusations of heresy. Wyclif and his followers, the Lollards, believed God should be made directly available to ordinary people, without the intercession of the clergy. The clerical hierarchy was so incensed that the Bishop of Norwich received permission from Rome to execute any Lollards he captured. Wyclif's followers were burned alive in a pit less than a mile from Julian's cell.

Meanwhile, the larger world beyond Norfolk and England was also in a state of upheaval. Five years before Julian was born, in 1337, the Hundred Years War between England and France had begun, and it would continue throughout her lifetime. The Great Schism split the Church in 1377, with one pope in France, the other in Rome.

And in the midst of all this, Julian came to believe unshakably that "all shall be well, and all shall be well, and all manner of things shall be well."

Julian's Writing

Julian's life as an anchoress gave her plenty of time to ponder the revelations she had received. She wrote first a short text, describing what she had seen on her sickbed, and over the next twenty years, as she further analyzed and meditated on her "showings," she wrote a longer text that vividly described all God had revealed to her.

Her book was the first to be written by a woman in the English language. At about the same time, Geoffrey Chaucer was also writing in the English of the era, but Chaucer had a sophisticated educational heritage Julian lacked. Her English was the ordinary vocabulary of common people. Some scholars believe she was unable to even read and write at the time of her revelation, and that she taught herself what she needed to know in order to record and pass on what God had shown her.

Julian's writing survived in copies made by nuns and guarded in convents. Because of the risk of being accused of heresy (an accusation not taken lightly during the Middle Ages), the book was not printed until 1670.

This Version of Julian's Text

The Norman Invasion had taken place three hundred years before Julian's lifetime, bringing a flood of new words into the Old English vocabulary. By Julian's day, English was rounding the corner from Middle English into the modern language we speak today. In the oldest manuscripts of Julian's book, the spelling is unfamiliar—but if you read the words out loud, you realize they are not as strange as they look.

There is much to be said for reading Julian in her original words, or in a modern translation that stays as true as possible to the original. Unfamiliar vocabulary can take us by surprise and strike us anew with a fresh awareness of its meaning. For instance, Julian used the word "one" as a verb, and speaks of "oneing ourselves with God" (rather than the

INTRODUCTION

Latin-based "uniting" we'd be more likely to use today); she also referred to the forces that "nought" us (bring us to nothing), rather than "negate" us.

Still, Julian wrote in the ordinary English of her day (rather than the Latin normally used by the educated upper classes for writing) because she believed her revelations were meant to be passed along directly to all people. She wasn't saying that vernacular English was *better* than the more erudite Latin in terms of its ability to express her meaning; she only wanted her readers to experience for themselves what she had experienced, a direct, one-to-one contact with God, without any clouding of its strength—and to do this she used words so familiar to her readers they would be nearly invisible, requiring no thought or effort to access their meaning.

It is with this in mind that I created this translation of Julian's book, a modern paraphrase of her text, using words that are as ordinary and accessible as possible (whether they come from Latin roots or Anglo Saxon), in order to present Julian's meaning most clearly to all twenty-first–century readers. In writing this, I relied on the edition of Julian's original words published by Pennsylvania State University Press (*The Writings of Julian of Norwich*, 2006), while making constant reference to etymological studies to dig back into what Julian would have truly meant when she used the words she chose. My etymological sources included *The Oxford English Dictionary*, Dr. Ernest Klein's *A Comprehensive Etymological Dictionary of the English Language* (1971), the *Barnhart Dictionary of Etymology* (1988), and the Online Etymology Dictionary. Using these sources as guides, I worked to get to the heart of Julian's meaning—and then offer it to modern readers as transparently as possible. For those readers interested in grappling for themselves with

Julian's words in her own language, I highly recommend the Penn State Press edition.

Language is constantly changing, and some words Julian used that seem familiar today actually had different nuances of meaning for someone living in the fourteenth century. For instance, "homely," a word Julian uses over and over in speaking of God, certainly did not mean Julian thought God was plain or unbeautiful. Instead, for Julian, *homely* meant "intimate"—in other words, something as familiar and comfortable as your home, the place where you feel most safe, most yourself—and it is this connotation I have expressed in my version of Julian's book.

Much of the religious language that has become the jargon of modern Christianity had its origins in the medieval period. Figures of speech that grew from the ordinary life of the Middle Ages (or the still more ancient Bible times) no longer have that same strength and liveliness today that they did when they were rooted in everyday experience. When we use these phrases, we think we know what we mean—but the meaning has faded and lost its energy. In some cases, a word's use has shifted so much that we lose sight of the spiritual truth that once underlay it.

The word "lord" is a good example of this. During the Middle Ages, the feudal hierarchy was the structure upon which society was built. It was necessary for the well-being and order of the community, as well as the safety of the individual. Today, we remember the hierarchy and often forget why it was necessary. To "lord it over someone" speaks of superiority versus inferiority, and we bring those connotations to any conversation with God in which we refer to the Divine as "Lord." But that meaning of the word did not show up in written English until the years just after Julian's death;

INTRODUCTION

in her day, the Old English word meant "keeper, guardian," and a lord's most vital function was to protect those under his care. Because of this, in this version of Julian's writings I have replaced the word "Lord" with "Protector." I believe this brings us closer to Julian's understanding of the word—and I hope the less familiar word will give us a fresh awareness of our relationship with Christ.

The word "passion" is another word that has come to mean something quite different today from what it did for Julian. The Old English word, still close to the surface in the fourteenth century, meant "endurance, patience, undergoing, bearing up under." The word did not take on the connotation of extreme emotion until the sixteenth century, and it wasn't connected to sexual emotion until even later. Consequently, throughout this version of Julian's book, I replaced references to Christ's Passion with a more modern term.

I spent a good deal of time pondering the best word to use. "Labor," in the sense of childbirth, is a good metaphor for the meaning Julian intended: Christ, like all pregnant women ready to deliver, committed himself to going through pain—and once committed, the only way out of the pain was to endure it, to keep going through to the other side. Like childbirth, Christ's death on the cross was a creative act in which physical agony played a necessary and unavoidable role; like childbirth, the outcome of Christ's pain and endurance was new life, a new life that made the pain all worthwhile. This meaning is essential to Julian's understanding of "passion," but without the connotation of childbirth, the word "labor" implies that the Cross was simply work Christ accomplished, a job he did; it does not contain passion's original meaning of being patient in suffering, of waiting out the pain. In the end, I opted for the phrase "Christ's Endurance." Again, I hope that by using a phrase that has not become a religious catchword, one with an awkward unfamiliarity that draws our attention, we will be startled into a new understanding of Christ's death.

Gender is also an issue I've addressed in my translation of Julian's showings. Julian was perfectly comfortable speaking of Christ as a mother, using the masculine pronoun to describe feminine aspects of the Divine. Modern feminist theology often claims Julian as one of its earliest proponents, but the term "feminism" would have meant nothing to Julian. Instead, she was totally focused on the Divine reality revealed during her mystical experience, a reality expressed through gender even as it transcended gender. Here again, I've endeavored to build into my translation of her book a similar transparency by using feminine pronouns where modern readers would be more comfortable using them, masculine pronouns where those make most sense—and using nongendered language where possible to be certain that the language I used to describe God is as inclusive as possible. Julian's English did not offer her this option, but ours does, and I believe that if Julian were writing today, she would gladly use inclusive language and extend some of her feminine metaphors for God to their more logical lengths. I've included additional notes at the beginning of Julian's chapters to indicate where I chose to change her original words, to further explain the choices I made, and to comment briefly on the deeper meanings found in Julian's ideas.

My translation is not intended for serious students of medieval theology; I have no desire to compete with the many far more scholarly and analytical works on Julian and her book. Instead, my goal is to allow ordinary readers to interact as simply and directly as possible with Julian's showings. She

INTRODUCTION

herself insisted that her individual story and identity were not important, that the only thing she wished to convey was the Divine message of love she had received (intended for everyone, not just for herself).

Julian wrote at the end of her book, "This book is begun by God's gift, by Divine grace, but I do not believe it has yet been finished. It is still developing and growing." I offer this modern-language translation of Julian's book in service to her lifelong labor: that her book will continue to grow and develop in the twenty-first century.

–Ellyn Sanna

A Revelation of Love in Sixteen Showings

This chapter is in effect Julian's table of contents. Here she outlines the entire book that follows.

Julian's reluctance to contradict the Church is immediately evident. In all likelihood, she was absolutely sincere in her devotion and commitment to the Church—but at the same time, the smoke and ashes from the Lollards' Pit (where Wyclif's followers were burned alive) would have blown through her window, a horrifying reminder of what happened to people who dared to contradict the Church.

In this chapter (and throughout the book), I have replaced the word "Savior" with "Rescuer." Savior has become a well-worn piece of Christian vocabulary, one we often say without considering the word's meaning. I've chosen to use a synonym instead, so that we can once again be confronted with the concrete and ordinary meaning of Christ's action in our lives. In the midst of despair and danger, the Divine Presence is with us—and we are rescued, kept safe, and set free.

This is a revelation of love that Jesus Christ, our endless joy, made in sixteen showings (sixteen particular and unique revelations).

The first of these showed me that His crown of thorns was precious and valuable, and along with this image came a unique understanding of the Trinity, the Incarnation, and the unity that exists between God and human beings. This showing and all the others that followed contained many lovely perspectives and lessons on God's wisdom and love; all sixteen showings are grounded and unified by this same viewpoint.

The second showing revealed the change in the color of Christ's beautiful face as a sign of His love-inspiring endurance on the Cross.

The third showed me that our Protector God, Almighty, All-Wisdom, and All-Love, not only created everything, but that the creative power of the Divine Essence continues to accomplish everything that happens.

The fourth showed me Christ's vulnerable body scourged and bloody.

The fifth revealed the Enemy overcome by Christ's love and endurance.

The sixth showed me our Protector bestowing honor on us as we are thanked in Heaven for our service to God.

The seventh revealed that our up-and-down emotions (from the heights of joy when we sense that our lives are lit up with grace—to the depths of depression when our physical lives seem to press down on us with a repulsive weight) matter little from a spiritual perspective. God's love and goodness keep us equally safe in our depression as in our joy.

A REVELATION OF LOVE IN SIXTEEN SHOWINGS

In the eighth showing, I saw Christ's last pains and cruel death.

The ninth showed me the joyful Trinity's pleasure in Christ's death, despite His physical pain and spiritual agony—and that Christ wants us to also be comforted and gladdened by His presence in this life until we experience Him in His fullness in Heaven.

During the tenth showing, our Protector Jesus revealed to me that His joyful heart is split in two by love.

The eleventh showed me Christ's love-worthy mother.

The twelfth revealed that our Protector God is the preeminent Being, that which rises above and before all else.

In the thirteenth showing, I realized that our Protector God wants us to appreciate and understand Divine achievement: how perfectly all things are made; the excellence of human beings; and the infinitely valuable work that has bridged our separation from God, turning all our guilt into nothing but endless worth. In this showing, our Protector said to me, "Look and see! I will use the same strength, wisdom, and goodness I used to accomplish humanity's safety and wholeness to make good all that is currently not good—and you will see it!" This is why God wants us to walk in faith, depending on the truth as revealed through the Church, since we can only occasionally see these secret things in the midst of this life.

The fourteenth showing is that our Protector is the ground in which our prayer is rooted and from which it grows. This shows us two sides of one coin: first is prayer (asking God for what we need), and the second is unshakeable trust (the confidence that God will answer us). When this coin is large (on both its sides), we are enriched; our prayer pleases God, and out of Divine goodness we are answered.

The fifteenth showing revealed to me that a moment shall come when we will suddenly spring out of all our pain and sadness into

Heaven's joy and fulfillment. There, our Protector Jesus will be our reward.

The sixteenth showing is this: the joyful Trinity, our Maker, dwells endlessly in our souls through Christ Jesus our Rescuer, even as Christ also honors and protects all things. In love, His strong and wise presence keeps us safe—and our Enemy shall never overcome us.

II
Three Gifts from God

Julian's longing for death, illness, and wounds may seem morbid to our modern ears. But unlike most of us today, she lived constantly in death's shadow. With more than half of her town's population destroyed by the Plague, the end of life would have become an ordinary and familiar acquaintance (though still heartbreaking). By identifying with Christ's death and making it the focus of her thoughts, Julian was struggling to find meaning in her reality.

Imagine if Julian had watched her husband and young children die, as well as many of her friends and extended family, while she alone survived. Where could she possibly seek comfort but from God? And would it not be completely understandable if she became obsessed with death? She no doubt wondered why she survived when so many had died, and "survivor guilt," as well as the longing to be closer to her lost loved ones, may have been what drove her to ask God for a serious illness, one that would help her better understand others' suffering. What apparently saved Julian from sinking into an unhealthy depression was her ongoing focus outside herself on Christ's experience of pain and death, a reference point from which to make sense of her own experiences.

These revelations were given to me, a simple, uneducated person, in the year 1373, on the thirteenth of May. I had always wanted God to give me three gifts: first, the mental attitude of Christ's endurance and death; second, physical illness by the time I was thirty years old; and third, to receive three wounds from God's other gifts.

As for my first wish, I thought I already had some feeling for Christ's endurance, but I longed for more by God's grace. I would have liked to travel through time so that I could be with Mary Magdalene and the others who were close to Christ; I wanted to see something with my physical eyes that expanded my awareness of our Rescuer's physical pain and the compassion of our Lady and all the others who loved Him and watched Him die. I wanted to be one of them; I wanted to suffer with them (on a physical level as well as a spiritual one). This was the only view of God I desired for now, in this life. I asked God for this gift, so that I might be better able to comprehend Christ's experience during His Endurance.

My sense of guilt inspired my second longing. I wanted to be sick enough to receive the Church's last rites, so sick that I myself would think I was dying and that everyone around me would think the same. I wanted to be stripped of this life's comforts. What's more, I wanted this sickness to give me the same physical and spiritual pains I would experience if I were actually to die, including all the storms and terrors of evil—everything except that actual leave-taking of my soul from my body. I hoped that after such a sickness, I would, by God's mercy, be scrubbed clean, so that my life would give God greater praise and I would be that much more ready for the time when I actually did die (for I wanted to be with God as soon as possible).

I set two conditions on these first two desires of mine, saying, "Protector God, You know what I long for, but I only want these things if they be Your will—and if they are not what You want, please don't be displeased with me, for I only want Your will for my life." I hoped to experience this sickness when I was thirty years old (the age at which Christ began His ministry).

As for my third request, God's grace and the Church's teaching had given me a deep longing to be wounded in three ways: first, to have my ego ground down into pieces; second, to be able to suffer with others; and third, to have a firm and unfailing desire for God's presence. I asked for all this without any conditions placed on my request at all.

My first two desires often dropped from my thoughts—but the third dwelled with me continually.

III
Suffering with Christ

Here, once again, Julian indicates that her primary concern lay outside herself: to gain a greater compassion for others' suffering. Her focus on Christ's death and the world to come was a natural outgrowth of her own experience, as well as a common characteristic of medieval religious thought in general.

Julian's visions are clearly a result of illness. Today, we might dismiss as delirium anything that came to our minds during a fever (and Julian herself has some of these same doubts), but the connection between sickness and revelation was accepted within the medieval mystical tradition. Julian implies throughout her book that God speaks to us in various ways, all equally legitimate: through our intellectual abilities, through our imaginations, and through the states of altered consciousness induced by illness, fasting, or even mental illness.

SUFFERING WITH CHRIST

When I was thirty and a half years old, God sent me a physical illness that lasted for three days and three nights. On the fourth night, I took the last rites, and I assumed I would die before day came. After this, however, I lingered on another two days and two nights; again on the third night, I thought I would die, and those who were with me thought so as well.

I was still young enough that I hated to think I was dying; and yet at the same time, there was nothing on Earth that motivated me to stay alive, and none of death's pains frightened me, for I trusted God's mercy. I only thought that if I could have lived longer, I would have gotten to know and love God better, and then I would have been able to know and love God even better when I reached Heaven's utter joy. I kept thinking that compared to Heaven's endless happiness, I had lived such a short, narrow life here on Earth that it seemed like nothing at all by comparison. Because of this, I thought, "Protector God, does my life no longer bring You praise?" My mind and my body told me I was about to die, and my mind was made up to give myself wholly, without reservation, to God's will.

I endured another day, but by then, my body was numb and paralyzed from the waist down. I asked to be set up, leaning back against the head of the bed, so that I could think more clearly during the time left to me. I wanted to be able to concentrate on God and whatever the Divine will was for me.

Since my end seemed so near, my curate was sent to be with me. By the time he came, I could not speak or move my eyes, so he set a cross in front of me. "I have brought you the image of your Protector and Rescuer," he said. "Look at it and find comfort."

My eyes had been turned up to Heaven, where I trusted I was going by God's mercy, but now I managed to shift my gaze to the crucifix. I thought I could endure looking straight ahead better than looking upward.

After this, though, my vision began to fail. The room seemed as dark as if it were night—except for the figure that hung from the Cross, which seemed to be lit with ordinary daylight, although I did not understand how that could be. Everything away from the Cross filled me with horror, as though thousands of demons hovered in the dark air.

After this, my upper body also began to lose feeling. I lacked nearly any physical sensation at all by this point, except for shortness of breath. And then I thought I had truly left this world.

But in this moment, suddenly, all my pain was taken from me, and I was as whole as I had ever been. The sudden change filled me with wonder; I thought it was some private, secret working of God's, rather than a natural occurrence. At the same time, this feeling of comfort did not convince me I would live, nor did it make me want to live. By now, I would rather have been completely freed from this world.

It occurred to me now that I should wish for the second wound from the Protector's generous gift: that I might experience the mental and physical sensations of Christ's Endurance. I wanted His pains to be my pains; I wanted to experience His compassion and His longing for God. As I wished for this, it never occurred to me that I might received a physical vision of God; I only wanted to experience the compassion and empathy Jesus demonstrated when He took on mortal flesh. It was for this reason that I wanted to suffer with Him.

The First Revelation

IV
Christ's Endurance and My Heart's Joy

This is the beginning of Julian's mystical "showing": the moment when the painted, inanimate crucifix apparently comes to life and bleeds blood that is "hot and fresh." This blood is for her a symbol of life rather than death.

Throughout her book, Julian often explains that some aspects of her revelation were seen with her physical eyes, while others were in her mind, as was the case with the image of Mary described here. Julian seems to consider both equally valid (and she also equally questions and tests the validity of both). In the modern world, we tend to distinguish between what is "imaginary" and what is "real" (what we can perceive with our senses, as per the scientific method, forgetting that our senses and our brains' perceptions can also be affected by circumstances). Shaped by medieval thought, Julian saw no such division.

At that moment, as I was still gazing at the crucifix, I saw red blood trickle down from under the crown of thorns. It was as hot and fresh as though the thorns had just been pressed onto the actual head of the One who was both Divine and human. I knew then with a rush of understanding that Jesus Himself was showing this to me, without any intermediary or translator.

At the same time, the Trinity filled my heart with a sudden joy. All at once, I knew what Heaven would be like—endlessly—for all those who come there. For the Trinity is God, and God is the Trinity; the Trinity is our Maker and Keeper, and through Jesus, the Trinity is our everlasting love and unending joy. I learned this in the first showing, and it was reinforced in the ones that followed, that wherever Jesus is, the Trinity is there as well.

"Bless God!" I shouted. I was filled with awe and wonder that the Divine One, who is so sacred, so terrifyingly holy, could be so familiar with a little creature of flesh and blood, treating me as though I were an equal.

I stored this revelation away in my mind, for I assumed that before I died, God would allow the devils to tempt me. I knew that this revelation of love and joy would give me all the strength I needed; it would give any living creature strength to face all Hell's temptations.

Next, God brought our blessed Lady to me in my mind. I had a spiritual vision of her physical appearance: an ordinary, humble girl, little more than a child, as she was when she conceived Jesus. I glimpsed the wisdom and integrity of her soul, and I understood how she kept her eyes fixed on her God and Maker, marveling with great reverence that the One who had made her would be born from her body. This wisdom and integrity—her awareness of her Maker's greatness and her own smallness—is what inspired her to say so humbly to the angel Gabriel: "Look, I am God's servant!" My vision of her made me understand that in her humbleness she is higher in worthiness and grace than all else that God made; in my opinion, the only thing higher than her total submission is Christ's incarnation as a human being.

V
The Hazelnut

Here, Julian affirms that God's presence is in everything that is good, and Divine love constantly encloses us. As the psalmist says, "Where can I go from your Spirit? . . . If I go up to the heavens, you are there; if I make my bed in the depths, you are there" (139:7,8 NIV). But Julian takes this a step further than what we usually hear: God *is* everything that is good, she writes. All life's pleasures and comforts are sacramental; they are God's hands touching us. In all of life's goodness, we come to know God, and through life itself, God's love encloses us as intimately and tangibly as the clothing we wear. And yet even as Julian affirms this, she also indicates she will never be completely at rest, never totally comfortable, until she is truly joined with God, with no "intermediary" aspect of Creation coming between her and the Divine.

This chapter also contains one of the most well-known images from Julian's writing: the hazelnut, a metaphor for both vulnerability and endurance, both smallness and an enormous potential for fertility. As I look at her hazelnut from my twenty-first–century perspective, I'm reminded of similar images used to explain the Big Bang theory. According to cosmologists, everything that is, the entire cosmos, was once a ball the size of a marble (or maybe a nut). In effect, this is the same meaning

THE HAZELNUT

Julian gives her hazelnut: the Little Thing is the whole of creation. Our entire complicated lives that seem so large and overwhelming are hidden in that tiny ball—and we in it are created, loved, and kept.

Julian's understanding of Divine love is practical, rooted in the material world, yet at the same time, she expresses a perspective here much like that found in Buddhism: we must encounter nothingness even in the midst of the created world. Our peace is built on detaching our hearts from all that God has created, so that we can rest only in God.

In Julian's original writing, she frequently uses the word *goodnes*, which I've chosen to supplement or replace with "unity." It would be easy to assume that Julian's concept equates to our modern "goodness," but in fact, the word has traveled through centuries, accruing a heavy layer of morality (of should's and ought-to's) along the way. Julian's "goodnes" was a simpler thing, built on Old English roots that had more to do with being gathered together, belonging together, united—a very different concept from that of our moralistic "goodness."

During this first showing, our Protector showed me a spiritual view of the Divine One's intimate love for us. I saw that the Divine Spirit is everything that is good, everything that comforts us and give us pleasure. This Spirit is our clothing. In love, the Divine One wraps us up, holds us tight, and encloses us with tenderness. The Spirit lives in everything good that we encounter, the entire universe, and we shall never be abandoned.

At the same time, the Spirit showed me a tiny thing the size of a hazelnut, as round as a ball and so small I could hold it in the palm of my hand. I looked at it in my mind's eye and wondered, "What is this?" The answer came to me: "This is everything that has been made. This is all Creation." It was so small that I marveled it could endure; such a tiny thing seemed likely to simply fall into nothingness. Again the answer came to my thoughts: "It lasts, and it will always last, because God loves it." Everything—all that exists—draws its being from God's love.

I saw that the Little Thing has three properties: First, God made it. Second, God loves it. And third, God keeps it; its ongoing existence depends on God. But to go further than that—to understand the actual relation of the Maker, the Keeper, and the Lover to my own being—I cannot understand. Until my very essence is united with the Divine, I will never be completely at rest, nor will I be totally happy until I am so firmly joined with God that there is nothing—no intervening or mediating aspect of Creation—between God and me.

We need to comprehend how small and inconsequential Creation is compared to God (who was never created but simply IS). When we perceive the nothingness in reality, we find God there. This is why our minds and souls are often restless and uncomfortable, because we rely on things that are so small, which can offer us no real rest or security, while we fail to realize that God is Almighty, All-Wise, All-Good. The Divine One is the essence of rest and security, the only true comfort. God wants to be known; the Divine One is pleased when we rest in the Spirit's presence, since all that was created will never be enough in and of itself to give us what we need. This is the reason why no soul finds peace until it achieves nothingness even in the midst of the created world. When we willingly, lovingly detach our minds from the world around us, we have the One who is all—and we find rest for our spirits.

Our Protector God also showed me the Divine joy when a soul comes, helpless, without any strength of its own, simply, intimately, with ordinary familiarity, into God's Presence. This is the soul's natural tendency when the Spirit touches it. This showing helped me understand this, and I said, "God, in Your goodness, give me Yourself, for You are enough for me. If I ask for less than You, then my life no longer worships You, and I am lacking. Only in You do I have everything."

These words express the soul's loveliness, and they come close to expressing the will of God, the will of goodness, for Creation. All Creation, all the Divine works, are contained within the Divine Unity, even as that Unity transcends all Creation. God is That-Which-Has-No-End, the source of Eternity, and we are made so that we are only complete when we are joined with the Divine. Although we have separated ourselves, with His Endurance Jesus restored our intimacy, and He keeps us safe in His love. And He does all this out of His goodness.

VI
Our Highest and Deepest Prayer

> Many of us grew up with the concepts that the world is evil, and that our bodies' cravings tend to be the source of this evil. We consider many of our most natural physical functions to be dirty and repugnant. Here, Julian insists that all the world's varied goodness is contained within the Unity of God—and then goes even further to say that each of our bodies' functions (even emptying our bowels) are vehicles for God's love.
>
> From this perspective, the spiritual life takes on a different tone. The most effective prayer technique, writes Julian, is simply to relax and let ourselves drop into that Unity, knowing that there all our longings will be satisfied, and our souls will "rush forward."

The purpose of this next showing was to teach our souls the wisdom of clinging to Divine Unity.

What came to my mind next was the way we pray: in our ignorance and incomprehension of love, we use many methods for asking God for what we want. But I realized now that God is worshipped—and delighted—when we simply turn to the Divine One, trusting totally in that Unity and clinging to Divine grace. This attitude reveals a deeper understanding of God and creates in us an unshakeable love, far more than any method of prayer our minds could contrive. Even if we were to practice all the prayer techniques ever used, they would never be enough to connect our souls to God with utter wholeness and fullness, for God's goodness is the entire whole of reality, a unity that lacks absolutely nothing. By focusing our attention here—on the absolute Unity that never fails—we achieve the truest form of prayer.

Along the same lines, it occurred to me that we pray to God because Christ became flesh and blood, because of His Endurance, because He loved us so much He was wounded and died, and because of the ways all this binds us to Him in endless life. And we pray to Him also for the sake of His mother's love, and because she helps us as well—but her love is just one more expression of God's Unity. And we pray because of the Cross where Jesus died—but all the strength and help that comes to us from the Cross is also contained within God's goodness and unity. And in the same way, the help we derive from the saints and all the rest of Heaven's company, the love and endless friendship they extend to us, that too is just one more expression of the goodness and unity of God.

For God's goodness is shown in a multitude of ways, each one lovely, but the most important expression is this: through a young girl's flesh, God took on human nature, and from that flows our redemption and endless safety. And that is why God is pleased when we seek and worship the Divine Presence in whatever way we can, understanding that God is the Unity in all things.

Resting in this Unity is the highest prayer, and it reaches down to our deepest needs. It brings our souls to life; it brings us more of life's fullness; and our lives expand with grace and strength. This attitude of prayer aligns most easily with our very natures, and it requires the least effort to achieve, for it is simply what our souls already crave, and what they shall always crave until we truly understand that we are wrapped in the Divine Unity: the goodness of God.

For God does not hold back from a single aspect of Creation, nor does the Divine One disdain to serve us in the simplest and most ordinary ways. Think how neatly our food is contained within our bodies, digested, and then is emptied out as needed, like a lovely drawstring purse that opens and closes. God is completely comfortable with all our bodies' activities; none of them offend the Divine Presence, for all our bodies' natural functions are Divine vehicles, filled with the love God bears us whose souls are made in the Divine likeness.

Just as our bodies are clothed with fabrics; our blood and muscles covered with skin; our bones wrapped with blood and muscles; and our hearts hidden at the center of all these—so are we, soul and body, clad in the goodness of God, completely enclosed and safe. Even more comforting is the reality of God's goodness, though, for our clothing, our flesh, our very bones, all may grow old and waste away—but the goodness and unity of God are always whole and strong. They are closer to us than our very bodies. Our Divine Lover longs for us to cling to God with all our strength, so that we may identify ourselves with goodness and unity forever. Of all the thoughts that may occupy our minds, this one pleases God the most, and it makes our souls rush forward toward wholeness.

Our souls are so beloved of the Highest One that nothing in Creation can completely comprehend how tenderly our Maker loves us. That is why, in grace and with Divine help, we can stand up straight as we use our spiritual vision, overwhelmed with endless awe for the boundless, immeasurable love God the Almighty shows us.

And that is why we may humbly ask our Divine Lover for whatever we want. For our natural and innate desire is for God—and God's desire is for us. Our longing will never end till at last, in complete and utter joy, we possess God's fullness. Then all our desires will be met.

The Divine will for us is that we love and know God, going as far as we can in this life, until the time when we can find complete fulfillment in Heaven. This is why God gave me this revelation, as well as all that followed, for the other showings all had their foundation in the first revelation.

Any time we look at our Maker with love, our importance in our own eyes diminishes, and we are filled with awe and humility and love for others.

VII
The Revelation of Faith

> In this chapter, Julian takes pains to make her description of the bleeding crucifix (which she claims to see with her actual "physical eyes") as detailed and concrete as possible; she wants her readers to be able to visualize as clearly as she did the sense-based physicality of her vision. The sensuality of her vision gives it an immediacy she connects to Christ's "hospitality"—his willingness to welcome us into the intimacy of his home.
>
> Julian also acknowledges here that our minds are not capable of constantly holding on to intense visions like hers—and yet the understanding we achieve in glimpses can remain "folded up" within our everyday, more prosaic faith.

To teach us this love was why (as best I can tell) our Protector God showed me Lady Mary in the same revelation—the wisdom and integrity that was hers simply because she looked with her whole heart at her Maker, a Being so limitless, so complete, so strong, and so good. Her vision of God was so great and high that she was filled with awe and saw herself as small and simple and poor by comparison. In other words, her clear view of her Protector made her complete in utter simplicity. On this foundation of humility was built her fulfillment, the grace that gave her strength and goodness beyond all other creatures.

All the while I was having these spiritual revelations, I was also seeing—with my physical eyes—the blood that dripped from Christ's head like red-brown pellets, as though His blood was squeezed out from His veins in tiny balls. The blood then spread bright red across His forehead, but as fast as it flowed, it always disappeared when it reached His eyebrows. As the revelation was unfolding, His blood kept dripping down, like rainwater falling from the eaves during a storm, so fast you could never hope to count the drops. The beads of blood that spread across His forehead were as round as herring scales.

All this seemed most significant to me, and the showing was so lifelike that it was horrifying and sweet, dreadful and lovely, all at the same time. I realized then that our God is also both terrifying and intimate, both awe-inspiring and courteous. This understanding filled me with comfort and gave me confidence.

As I sought to comprehend the vision more fully, God brought to my mind this example: Imagine the most regal king or lofty lord who wants to honor one of his servants. He does so by making himself at home with the servant, by being an intimate friend with him, both in public and private. This ordinary intimacy honors—and pleases—the servant far more than if the king had given him great wealth and rich gifts but held himself distant all the while.

That is how it is with our Protector Jesus and us. He who is the strongest, highest, and worthiest Being chooses to be intimate with us in utter simplicity, humility, and courtesy. Christ is the embodiment of Divine intimacy with humanity. This amazing joy belongs to each of us; one day we shall all experience it totally, when we come into His presence.

That is why our Protector wants us to seek Divine grace and help with such joy and delight, receiving comfort and strength until the moment we experience God totally. In my opinion, this is the most complete joy we shall ever know: the amazing familiarity and hospitality God our Maker and Christ our Brother and Rescuer extend to us.

None of us can completely experience this marvelous intimacy in this life, unless the Protector gives us a special revelation or the Holy Spirit bestows on us an unusual amount of internal grace. But although we may not know the full experience in this life, we can claim it in faith and love, for it is in faith, hope, and love that our lives are rooted and made firm.

This showing, which I am sharing with whomever God wants, teaches all this plainly. It is nothing new, merely an unfolding of the faith we already share, with many of its secrets opened and revealed. But extraordinary revelations like these can only occupy our minds for a small space of time; once that time has passed, the revelation's secrets may be folded up and hid once more—and yet by faith and the Spirit's grace, we can keep all we have learned for the rest of our lives. The vision I received is neither less nor more than the faith we have always had, as will be made clear as I describe the rest of what was shown to me.

VIII
Sharing in Love

> Julian gives us here a six-point outline for this first showing, and then she underlines her belief that her vision was given not merely to her but to all of us—and that the Divine goal in doing this was that we would experience more deeply the joy God wants for us all.

All the while, as I watched the blood flowing from Christ's head, I could not stop saying, "Bless God!"

In this showing, I understood six things: First is the physical token of Christ's Endurance, as seen in the flow of His blood from His head. Second is the loveable young girl who became His mother. The third is the joy of God, the One who was, is, and ever shall be, All-Strength, All-Wisdom, and All-Love. The fourth is the totality of what God made, for I knew how great and wide, beautiful and good Creation is, despite how small it appeared to me when I saw it compared to the Maker-of-All. Fifth is the fact that God's love created all things, and Divine love keeps all things in existence, and it shall keep everything forever; not one thing made shall ever be lost. The sixth is that everything that is good is God; whatever goodness we experience in this life is truly a taste of God, for it *is* God.

All these things our Protector showed me in the first showing. I had all the time and space I needed to experience and comprehend these revelations. The physical vision faded away in time, but the spiritual insights continued to dwell in my mind. I rested in awestruck joy, yearning to see more, if I dared, or else, if it were God's will, to look at this same vision for an even longer time.

During this experience I felt my love for others come awake, and I longed to share with them my experiences, for I knew how much comfort this revelation would give them. I turned to those who were in the room with me and said, "This is my Judgment Day." I meant that I was about to die, and I wanted my companions to understand how short life is so they would use the time they had to love God more. I was assuming I was about to die, and I was filled with a desperate wonder, a sense of both awe and despair. I thought the revelation God had just given me was for the benefit of those who would continue in this life. Even now, I know that all I say as I describe my vision was meant for others as much as for me.

That is why I ask you not to focus on me, the one who received the vision, but on what the vision shows you. With strength, wisdom, and humility, focus on God, allowing the Divine One to enrich you with gentle love and endless goodness. The showings are not mine; they are all of ours. Help yourself to the comfort and joy they offer as though God had sent them to you directly. God wants to make you happy!

IX
God Is Everything That Is Good

Julian stresses here that she is claiming no extraordinary relationship with God. As she repeatedly insists, her visions are intended to merely make more clear to us the faith we already have, not replace it with something new. She skirts around the issue of universal salvation versus the Church's teachings regarding sin and Hell by saying simply that her vision did not show her anything regarding the damned, only the redeemed.

In this chapter, Julian also stresses the active ongoing role the reader has in relation to her visions. Although we speak of the "Showings of Julian of Norwich," she never claimed them as "hers"; instead, she assumes the visions are for all of us, and that God will continue to make them clear to us, even beyond her writing.

This showing from God only makes me good in so much as it inspires me to love God more. And if it helps you love God more, then the revelation proves more about you than it does about me. I'm not saying this for the benefit of those who are already wise (because they will already know it), but I'm saying this to comfort you whose thoughts may not have gone so deep before. I want you to relax in the knowledge that we all share the same comfort.

My experience does not mean that God loves me more than anyone else, even the smallest soul. I'm sure that many people who go through their lives with only the Church's ordinary teachings to guide them, who never experience a supernatural vision of God's love, still love God more and follow the Divine One more closely than I do. Whenever I look at myself as if I stand alone in the midst of Creation, I see how insignificant I am—and yet, when I take my place in the Body, I am united in love with all others who follow Christ.

Humanity finds its saving life in this unity. For God is everything that is good; the Divine One has made and loves all reality. This is the Body, and when a human being loves others in that Body, she is loving all Creation. Contained within redeemed humanity is everything—all Creation and its Maker—for God is in humanity, and God is in all, and so everything is united into a single Body. It's my hope that by God's grace, anyone who can see from this perspective will be enlightened and comforted.

I am speaking now of those human beings who are redeemed, for during my visions, God did not show me any others. I am not seeking to deny anything the Church teaches. By God's grace, I keep those teachings firmly in sight, and I will never intentionally deny them. This was my viewpoint as I studied the revelation

I'd been given; during the entire showing, I perceived that God's message to me and the message revealed through the Church were one and the same.

All this was shown to me in three ways: through my physical eyes, through my intellectual understanding, and through spiritual visions. I wish I could describe the spiritual visions more clearly and explicitly, but I trust our strong Protector God will reveal to each of you the meaning of these visions more sweetly and deeply than I could ever explain them.

The Second Revelation

X
Seeking Versus Seeing

> Julian's second showing begins with still more detailed images of the dying Christ. She tells us she was seeing with her physical eyes and that all the while she was longing to see more clearly. From her experience (one that at first seemed too trivial to her to be worthy of being considered a "revelation"), she draws the conclusion that this paradox (seeing God/not seeing God; having God/yearning for God) is a central (and normal) aspect of the human journey. Seeking God and seeing God are equally valuable, Julian affirms. We do not need to worry if we feel we cannot "find" God, for we are only responsible for seeking; no formula exists for finding. The revelation of the Divine Presence is always unpredictable and surprising.

After this, I perceived with my physical eyes the face on the crucifix that hung before me. I gazed at it continually, seeing a portion of His Endurance, a love that never failed despite the spitting, insults, and blows He received. The face changed color as I watched. Once, I saw half the face, beginning with the ear, covered with dried blood. Then the other half was covered, while the blood on the other side of the face vanished.

These were physical perceptions, but they came to me as though through darkness and clouds. I longed to be able to see more clearly, but then I reasoned, "If God wants to show you more, then the Holy Spirit will be your light. You need no other source of illumination. And since you are looking at the Son of God even now, then you will have the light you seek."

In this world, we are so blind and ignorant that we fail to seek the Divine Presence until It is revealed to us. As soon as we catch a glimpse of God, however, grace stirs us, and we yearn to see yet more clearly and joyfully. And so I both saw God, and at the same time I longed to see God; I had God, even as I yearned for God. This is the way our lives go; this is the way they are meant to go while we are in this life.

At one point, my imagination brought me to the bottom of the sea. There I saw green hills and valleys, their stones draped with moss—and I understood that if anyone were under the water and saw God there, she would be safe, both body and soul. Even beyond that safety, she would experience more comfort and peace than this world would ever understand.

God wants us to believe that we do in fact see the Divine Presence continually, even though we feel as though we barely catch a glimpse of God. Our belief fills our lives with grace. In the end, God will be seen—and God will be sought; God will give us rest—and God will be trusted.

This second revelation was so small, simple, and humble, that I was troubled by it. I felt sad, worried, and full of yearning, for I could hardly believe that it was actually a revelation from God. But later, our good Protector gave me greater insight, and I understood that this was truly a Divine vision, though it was only the shape and likeness of the foul, dead skin humans wear in this life, the dying flesh our lovely, bright Protector bore for us.

It reminded me of Veronica's handkerchief, where Christ's own face appeared, for I too saw His face as it was in the midst of His agony on the Cross. I saw His resolution to go to His death; I saw the way His face changed color as He suffered. The image was so dark, so gaunt, so sorrowful, that it hardly seemed possible this was the same face that is Heaven's highest loveliness, Earth's fairest flower, and the sweetest fruit from a human womb. So how could the image I saw be so discolored and ugly?

I will explain how God's grace gave me understanding of this paradox. By faith we know—and through the teaching of the Church we believe—that the blessed Trinity made humanity in God's image. In the same way, we know that when human beings fell so far from God's love, the only way we could be restored to what we had been called to be was through the One who made us. The One who made human beings in love would use the same love to bring us back to even greater joy and unity. And just as we were made like the Trinity at Creation when we first came into being, when we are remade, our Maker wants us to be like Jesus Christ, our Rescuer, with Him in Heaven for eternity.

But between these two goals—our initial Divine likeness and then our Christ-likeness—lies the step Jesus took when, out of love and reverence for human beings, He made Himself like us; He wore our skin. When He did this, He not only shared humanity's best qualities; He also took on our mortality, our pain, and all our ugliness, so that we could become guiltless, restored to innocence. Jesus' bright loveliness was hidden inside our dying flesh. And yet I dare say no human being was ever as beautiful as He was until His beauty was discolored by the sorrow and ordeal of His death. (The eighth showing speaks more on this subject.)

This second vision was dim and cloudy, but it teaches us that God is pleased when we seek the Divine Presence continually, even if from our perspective, we do nothing but seek and suffer. We see with clarity that we have found God only when the Spirit's special grace reveals this to us. It is the seeking, with faith, hope, and love, that pleases our Protector, while it is the finding that pleases us and fills us with joy.

All this made me realize that during this time that we suffer on Earth, seeking is as good as seeing. Leave your awareness of the Divine Presence up to God, in humility and trust, to reveal to you as God wants. Our only job is to cling to God with total trust. Whether we see God or only seek to see God, I believe we add to the Divine Essence when we simply fasten our minds and lives onto God.

These are the two actions this vision teaches: seeking and seeing. Everyone seeks God in his own way, as the Spirit's grace allows, and the Church's teachings help us with this. God wants our seeking to have three elements: First, that we seek diligently, without giving in to laziness, and—as much as is possible—without depression and empty anxiety. Second, that we discipline ourselves to rest in Divine love, without complaining or struggling against God's work in our lives, with the realization that our lives on the Earth are only temporary. And third, that we trust God totally with all our strength. God wants us to understand that the sudden and joyful appearance of the Divine in our lives will take us by surprise.

For the Divine works in hidden ways, and yet at the same time, God wants us to perceive the Holy Presence in our lives. When this Presence comes to us, it comes out of the blue, with such speed that we are startled—and God wants us to trust and wait for this Divine Jack-in-the-Box. For God is utterly kind, and the Holy Presence welcomes our hearts with total hospitality. Blessed may God be!

The Third Revelation

XI
The Midpoint

In this chapter, Julian first refers to God as a "Point" or the "Midpoint," a concept she comes back to again in later chapters. If, as some scholars believe, she was originally an uneducated woman, this concept alone, based as it is on Euclid's geometry, would indicate her education had advanced substantially by the time she wrote this portion of her book. (If she was self-educated, as seems likely, her achievement becomes even more impressive.) She may also be making reference here to the writings of Pseudo-Dionysius (a fifth-century theologian) and Boethius (another fifth-century Christian), both of whom spoke of God as the One who unites at the center all the radii of a circle.

This concept shows up elsewhere as well, in the images of both poets and scientists. Dante Alighieri, writing in Italy at about the same time Julian was creating her book in England (though it's unlikely these two creative thinkers ever read each other's works), also referred to a point in his *Paradiso*: "Heaven and all nature hangs upon that point" (xxviii. 16). In Dante's *Vita Nuova*, Love says, "I am as the center of a circle, to which all parts of the circumference bear an equal relation." In the twentieth-century, psychologist Carl Jung described the psychic journey in similar terms: "The One is the midpoint.

> ... I saw that everything, all the paths I had been following, all the steps I had taken, were leading back to a single point." The twentieth-century poet T.S. Eliot also echoes Julian when he describes in "Burnt Norton" of *The Four Quartets* the "dance" that exists at "the still point of the turning world." And physicists speculate that at the moment of the Big Bang, the entire universe burst into existence from one singularity, a single point of zero size.
>
> Julian's theology often seems radical, but it too has it's echoes in others' writing. Her description of sin as nothingness, the absence of reality, for example, is also found in the work of other theologians, including both the early Christian father Augustine and the twentieth-century author C. S. Lewis. Aristotle's concept of the unmoved mover, the still point from which all motion sprang, is similar to Julian's discussion of God as Divine Verb, but Julian goes further to indicate that the Divine Force not only set the world in motion but continues to be present in all action.

Next, in my mind's eye I saw God contained in a tiny particle, a Point so infinitesimal it could barely be seen and yet it contained the origin and essence of all things. This vision made me realize that God is truly in all reality.

As I looked at this vision and comprehended it, I was filled with a vague anxiety, and I thought, "What is sin?"

For I saw that even the smallest, most trivial action is actually God at work. Nothing is done by accident, coincidence, or chance; everything happens as part of God's wise pattern. What we perceive as coincidence merely looks so because our vision is so limited, our perspective so hampered. Things that take us by surprise have actually existed endlessly in God's ongoing wisdom (which constantly works to achieve what is best for us). In our blindness, we exclaim, "What a coincidence!" or "It was such good luck!" But from God's perspective, things look quite different.

The only conclusion I can draw from this is that whatever happens, happens for good—for God is at work in all things. In this vision (where I perceived the Point of all life, both its origin and its purpose), I did not see the action of the created world but only God's action taking place in Creation. God is the Midpoint of all things, the center on which the world turns. I was convinced God did all things well, for sin—the separation from love—can by definition have no part in the Divine Essence.

At this point, I saw that sin is nothing. All action is God, and sin is no action at all. God is all reality, and sin is the absence of reality. The Point I saw was all reality, and it contained no sin, no separation from God or the love that sustains the world. As I grasped this knowledge, I set it aside, so that I could focus on Christ and whatever He wanted to show me next.

And so, as much as I was capable of absorbing in that space of time, I saw the rightfulness of God's action in the world. Right-full-ness has two beautiful qualities: it is right and it is full. It goes directly toward its goal, drawing a straight, true line, and it needs no help to get there, neither mercy nor grace, for it is sufficient in itself. As a result, God's actions cannot fail. (But on another occasion, which I shall describe later, God gave me a showing that revealed the bare facts about sin—and in that situation, mercy and grace have their place.)

I believe this vision was given to me because God wants to sharpen our focus on the Divine Essence in particular and Divine works in general. For the Divine actions are full of goodness; they are acts that are comfortable and pleasant. They give the soul elbow-room; they bring a sense of comfort to anyone who turns from blind human viewpoints to the lovely and joyous Divine perspective.

Human beings consider that some acts are good while others are evil, but that is not how God looks at things. All that exists was made by God, and so, in essence, all actions are God's doing. It is easy to understand that good deeds—what we consider to be high and moral actions—are well done, but from God's perspective, the highest level of action and the lowest are equally well done. For God has ordained the Divine Essence in each thing that exists, and all actions are simply a going forth of that Essence. And that is why there is no Doer but God. God is the only Verb, the single Action that moves through every human and earthly deed.

The Divine purpose never changes, nor will it ever change, world without end. All things that exist have always existed in God's mind; there is no beginning to God's thoughts. Each and every thing was set in order before anything was made; each piece of the real world stands true forever. Nothing whatsoever shall ever fall into nothingness. God made all things complete and good—and therefore, the blessed Trinity constantly delights in the totality of the Divine work.

All this God showed me with utter joy, as if to say: "See! I am God. See! I am in all things. See! I do all things. See! I never lift My hands from Creation, nor shall I ever, world without end. See! I complete all things, leading them to the goal I have ordained for them without any beginning, by the same strength, wisdom, and love through which I created them. How can anything be wrong with the world, when all this is the case?"

In this way, my soul was tested and strengthened throughout this vision with courage, wisdom, and love. I saw that it would truly be to my advantage to go along with its message and reverently give myself over to enjoying God.

The Fourth Revelation

XII
Christ's Blood Is Love's Bounty

> Like many other people of faith in the Middle Ages, Julian was comfortable using physical images to think about spirituality. Although Christians still speak of the saving power of Christ's blood (particularly in Evangelical circles), they are unlikely to envision that blood as graphically as Julian does here. What Julian is really saying, though, when she speaks of Christ's blood flowing between all worlds and times, is that the Incarnation—God manifested in a body filled with the same life-giving red and white blood cells, plasma, and platelets that flow in every human being—transformed reality, in the past, now, and forever, both on Earth and in Heaven, and in every unseen realm of reality.

After this, I saw the image of Christ seem to bleed from the scourging He received. As His sweet body was beaten, His beautiful skin split open, revealing His tender flesh. So much blood flowed from Him that I could see neither skin nor wound; He seemed to be made completely of blood. But after the blood had flowed down His body, before it could drop into the air, it disappeared. There was so much blood that I knew I needed to pay attention to it and consider what it meant. If physical blood had been flowing in my room (rather than the blood of a spiritual vision), it would have covered my bed and spilled over onto the floor.

It occurred to me then that God has created abundant water on the Earth, and that this water that serves us in so many ways is a love token from God—and yet as dependent as we are on the Earth's water, God wants us to be more intimately dependent on Christ's blood. His lifeblood—His essence—washes away our selfishness better than any earthly bath, and this same essence is the drink that refreshes our souls more than any other. His blood is as plentiful as it is valuable; through His love it becomes our own lifeblood, filling us with joy.

Look and see! In our world, precious things are often rare, and as a result, there is never enough to go around. But that's not the way it works with Christ's blood, which is so precious in part *because* it is so bountiful. This infinitely valuable abundance could not be contained by this world, and so it overflowed into Hell, where it burst Hell open and delivered all who were separated from God and brought them home to Heaven. This life essence will wash all Creation (past, present, and future), restoring it to unity with God. The cherished bounty streams upward as well, from Earth to Heaven, where it continues to flow from Christ as He prays for us to the Father. This stream of life will continue for as long as it is needed. In all the realms of Heaven, in all the worlds, it flows, and all reality is enriched by humanity's restoration. Those who have lived in the past, those who are living now, and those who will live in the future are all revitalized by this life-giving blood; not one from that number will miss out on the life it gives.

The Fifth Revelation

XIII
Christ's Death Overcomes the Enemy

> Julian expresses her belief in the Fiend—Satan—in this chapter, and yet she insists that even though evil is real, we are to pay no attention to it but instead focus completely on all that is good, that is God. We can dismiss the forces of evil with resolute laughter.

Before God gave me any words for my experience, the Divine Spirit impressed on me that I needed to merely pay attention, simply absorbing for now the concepts, without analysis. Then, silently, these words formed in my consciousness: "This is how the Fiend is overcome." This was said in reference to the vision of the Cross I had just experienced.

Our Protector revealed that the Fiend feels the same malice as he did before the Incarnation. His work is useless now, however, for no matter how much he labors, he continually sees souls escape his grasp by virtue of Christ's Endurance. This is his misery, for although God allows him to work in our world, each of his actions is turned to joy by Divine action. He might as well not do anything at all, for his efforts come to nothing. All his strength is absorbed by God and turned to good.

As best I can tell, there is no cruelty or anger in God, for our good Protector works endlessly to bring us into relationship with the Divine. God wants only to do good to us as we are restored to unity with the Spirit. With strength, determination, and utter integrity, Christ withstands the forces of evil and all their efforts to undo the Divine purpose. I saw too that our Protector simply laughs at the Enemy's malice; in God's eyes, the Fiend is nothing, and God wants us to have this same perspective.

I couldn't help but laugh out loud when I saw this. My laughter was contagious, and everyone who was in my room with me began to laugh too. This laughter made me so happy that I wished everyone everywhere could see what I had seen and join our laughter.

But I did not see Christ laugh as He hung on the cross. This made me understand that we may laugh in relief and joy that the devil is overcome, but when I say I saw our Protector laugh at the Enemy, it was an internal revelation of the truth; there was no change in Christ's mood. For God is always the same. The Divine Spirit experiences no emotional ups and downs.

My own mood turned more serious now, and I said, "I see three things—a source of communal amusement and pleasure, a thing to be scorned, and a resolute truth. I perceive this as a sort of game, because the Fiend is overcome; this is a game whose rules ensure that we are joyful winners. I also see that the Fiend is to be merely dismissed with contempt from our consciousness, for this is how God looks at him. And at the same time I see the passionate determination Christ showed on the Cross; His agony was no joke, but rather a resolute labor of total commitment."

We see with a double vision, things as they are now and things as they will be in Eternity, but God sees both perspectives united. And that is why God perceives the Enemy as nothing, for the End of Time shall bring the Fiend's destruction. He looked at human beings with malice, but in the end, his troublemaking will come to nothing. All the Earth's woe and pain shall be transformed into endless joy. And the Earth's hardships and sorrows, along with the Enemy who worked this evil, will be thrown away into nothingness and hidden from our sight forever.

The Sixth Revelation

XIV
Our Affirmation in Heaven

> Throughout her book, Julian speaks of both Divine familiarity and Divine courtesy. "Courtesy" was a concept brought to England by the Normans; it was the knight's sense of honor, integrity, and deferential service. The two concepts, familiarity and courtesy, are at opposite ends of a continuum: the one has to do with the intimacy found between ordinary people who share a home, while the other implies the courtly stateliness of nobility. In this chapter, as Julian speaks of how we will be greeted when our lives on Earth are completed, she gives us an image of God that unites these two disparate concepts into a single picture of welcome and love.

After this, our good Protector said to me, "Thank you for your hard work. Thank you especially for giving Me your youth."

And in this next showing, my consciousness was lifted up into Heaven, where I saw our Christ as a homeowner who has called all His beloved servants and friends to a formal dinner, a stately celebration. I realized our Protector did not take His place at the table; instead, He was present everywhere, making sure all His guests were always comfortable and enjoying themselves. He treated His guests with such courtesy and welcome, singing them a song of endless love, that His essence filled His home—filled the Heavens—with joy and delight.

God showed me that every soul in Heaven—those who served God to even the slightest degree on Earth—shall experience three levels of joy. The first arises when God thanks us for our earthly efforts. This honor is so great that we will feel as though we have no room for any other joy. It seemed to me that the entirety of human pain could never merit such honor, and yet God extends to us Divine gratitude. Our second level of joy rests in the fact that all Creation shall see how God welcomes us and thanks us for our work on Earth. The example that came to mind is of a king who says thank you to his servants. His thanks alone is a great honor, but if he broadcasts his gratitude to the entire realm, then the honor is still greater. And the third level is this: our joy in God's gratitude and affirmation shall continue, as new and glad as it was when we first received it, forever and ever. We will never get used to the honor God does us.

I saw that each person's age shall be made known in Heaven with a sweet intimacy and familiarity, thus honoring each one for how she used the time she was given. Those who willingly and freely offered their youth to God are thanked with special reverence.

But it did not matter how long a man or woman had turned toward God on Earth, whether for an instant, a day, or an entire lifetime. In the end, each person experiences all three levels of joy. The more aware we are of the welcome and courtesy with which Divine Love reaches out to us, the more eager we are to serve God all the days of our lives.

The Seventh Revelation

XV
Fleeting Sorrow, Constant Peace

> Not all of Julian's showings were supernatural visions. During this one, she experienced only a rapid cycle of up-and-down emotions, flip-flopping between despair and joy. She understood this to be a Divine object lesson, letting her know that our emotions are neither punishment nor reward, but simply different forms of "God's gifts." They are meant to drive us forward in our spiritual lives, but they do not reveal to us the true nature of eternal reality, for we are kept "equally safe in sadness and in happiness."

After that, a spiritual delight filled my soul. I was made complete with the certainty that the Divine holds all things firm and constant, forever and ever. This assurance was so strong, so glad, so spiritual, that I was completely at peace, totally at rest. Nothing on Earth could bother me.

But this feeling only lasted a while—and then I turned inward on myself, feeling heavy and weary. I was so irritated with myself, so impatient, that I was tired of my life. I could think of nothing that offered comfort or ease of mind—only faith, hope, and love. I had these in reality, but I could barely feel them.

And then again, our Protector gave me once more the same comfort and rest for my soul, so satisfying, so sure, so joyful, so strong, that no worry, no sorrow, no physical pain could have distressed me then.

But the cycle continued: my emotions would sink, and I would be overwhelmed with pain—and then once more joy and pleasure would lift me up—and then again, my mood would drop. Up and down, up and down: I must have ridden this emotional seesaw about twenty times. While I was filled with joy, I could have said with Saint Paul, "Nothing can separate me from the love of Christ!"—and when I was overcome with emotional pain, I might just as easily have said with Peter when he tried to walk on water, "Protector, save me! I'm about to perish!"

As best I can understand, the purpose of this vision was to show that our souls are driven forward by the emotional cycles we all experience: sometimes we are comforted, and sometimes we feel we have been abandoned. God wants us to understand that our emotions are not reality. The Divine One keeps us equally safe in sadness and in happiness.

Sometimes, it is good for us to feel as though we have been left to ourselves. These feelings of separation from God are not always caused by sin, I realized, because how could I have sinned during my experience of this showing? The shift from joy to despair was too sudden for me to have had a chance to sin!

Nor have we earned the joy we experience. Both sorrow and elation are God's gifts to us through our emotions. The Divine hands are always outstretched to us with good things God wants to give. God allows us to feel a range of emotions—but they are all expressions of Divine love.

FLEETING SORROW, CONSTANT PEACE

God wants us, even in the midst of our pain and sadness, to hold on to peace with all our strength. Ultimately, our joy will never end, but our sorrow is fleeting. All sadness will evaporate into nothingness for those who are restored to unity with God. That is why, when we experience depression and anxiety, we should not allow our minds to dwell on these feelings. Like any temporary pain, these sensations are to be endured until they pass—and then we can move on once more to the endless enjoyment God offers us.

The Eighth Revelation

XVI
A Portion of Christ's Endurance

> This chapter and the one that follows may seem particularly morbid to our modern sensibilities. But once again, what Julian is describing in these chapters is the reality of the Incarnation: the Divine presence embodied even in physical agony, even in death and decay.

After this, Christ showed me the time when He was near death on the Cross. I saw His sweet face look dry and pale, as though all the blood had left it. Then it grew still more pale, dead, with all its life force gone . . . then the flesh turned blue . . . then a duller blue, as He sank deeper into death. I could see His Endurance most clearly in His face, as it shifted colors, especially in His lips. The change in His face—from beautiful, flushed, and fresh, to pale, then dark with death—caused me great pain. His nose withered and collapsed into His face, and His body turned brown and black. The bright colors of life drained from Him, leaving Him desiccated and dying. While I watched, it seemed to me that a harsh cold wind was blowing around the Cross, and all the while His precious life force drained from His sweet body—and yet I still saw moisture in His flesh.

But His pain and the flow of blood from inside His body combined with the cold and the wind outside and worked together against Him. These four forces—two external and two internal—dried Christ's flesh as time went by. His pain was sharp and bitter, and yet it never let up. I watched as all the spirit evaporated from Him, leaving His flesh lifeless, and yet as long as any life force lingered, His pain endured.

This long torture seemed to me to last for seven days, as though for seven long nights He lingered on the point of death, dying but not dead, suffering the agony of His final pain and never being released. His body was so discolored, so shrunken, so desiccated, that He seemed to have been dead for seven days—and yet He was enduring the agony of death all the while. I thought surely this must be the end of His agony.

XVII
Ultimate Pain

Reading this description of the crucified Christ is no more pleasant than watching Mel Gibson's explicit portrayal of the Crucifixion in his 2004 movie *The Passion of the Christ*. When the movie was criticized for portraying violent torture in a needlessly brutal and relentless way, Gibson insisted his intention had been to confront viewers with the intensity of Christ's self-sacrifice. His perspective is at odds with most modern portrayals of the Crucifixion. Protestant Christians have even removed Christ's body from their crosses, as though to sanitize and spiritualize the meaning of Christ's death.

By contrast, in the Middle Ages, gruesome portrayals of the Crucifixion were common both in written text and visual art. The Church considered these to be effective tools for eliciting an emotional response that encouraged believers to identify more deeply with Christ. These graphic images were not so shocking, however, to viewers living in a world where death was commonplace. In the modern world, we have done our best to hide death out of sight, and the mortuary business prettifies our loved ones' dead bodies before we can bear to look at them. Medieval society, on the other hand, was well accustomed to casually confronting death's ugliness. Not only did most people die at home, but dead criminals hung rotting at crossroads and on city gates, and the corpses of Plague victims were carried through the streets in wheelbarrows. It is within this context that Julian wrote.

In the end, as repugnant as we may find Julian's description, it forces us to confront the sheer physicality of the Incarnation. The Incarnation was not symbolic and spiritual, insists Julian: it was real, to the point that the Divine entered even the human body's most disgusting and terrifying moments.

As I watched Christ's death continue before my eyes, His words came to my mind: "I thirst." I saw then in Christ two kinds of thirst: one physical and one spiritual. (I shall speak of His spiritual thirst in chapter XXXIII.) For now, I focused on His physical thirst, that which was caused by the lack of moisture in His body.

His life-giving flesh and bones were drained of blood and moisture. As He hung from the nails that pierced His tender flesh, the weight of His body wrung the life from Him, leaving His body dry and shriveled. The nails were so large that as He sagged there, hour after hour, they tore great wounds in His flesh. The crown of thorns pressed on His head, ripping holes in His skin, and these became caked with dried blood; His sweet hair tangled in the thorns, and the flesh of His scalp dried and cracked. The vulnerable skin of His head had pulled loose from the bone and hung like a tattered cloth, and now, it sagged over His skull as though it would fall off altogether. Its heavy looseness filled me with dread and sorrow, but I realized that the crown of thorns fastened His skin to His head, like clothes hung on the line to dry. There seemed no end, no bottom, no limit, to the torture He endured.

This sight continued awhile, but soon it began to change. The garland He wore of thorns became circled with another garland of blood, and both of these turned brown, like the color of an old scab. His skin now appeared tan and shriveled, like a dry board that has been aged, and His face was a darker brown than His body.

During this showing, I saw that Christ's dryness had four causes: First, His body was nearly bloodless from His wounds. Second, pain had wrung all moisture from Him. Third, He had been hung up in the wind, the way you might spread out a wet towel to dry. And fourth, when He asked for water, He received none. Oh, His pain was so terrible! But the dryness He endured, the terrible thirst and shriveling of His life, that seemed to me to be the worst of His agonies.

I watched while He endured the pain of death, and at the same time was forced to suffer the terrible cold as the wind evaporated all moisture from His flesh. And as for His other pains—they were so great I have no words to describe them.

His pain in turn filled me with pain. I knew His pain was in the past; He had only suffered on the Cross once, but I knew He was showing it to me, granting my wish. And during all this I felt no pain but Christ's. I realized then how little I had known when I'd asked to experience Christ's pain. If I had understood how great that pain actually was, I would never have been able to pray as I had. For I felt as though this pain was the greatest I had ever experienced.

I thought: "Is there any other pain as bad as this?" And the answer filled my brain: "Hell is a pain that's worse than this, for in Hell there is also despair. But of all pains that lead eventually to healing, this is worst, to see Love suffer." How could any pain be greater than to see the suffering of the One who is all my life, all my joy, all my well-being? And as I thought this, I felt that I truly loved Christ more than myself, and that no pain I might experience could be as bad as the sorrow of watching His pain.

XVIII
His Pain Is Ours

> Julian writes in this chapter of Saint Dennis of France, who actually was martyred in 250, and so could not have been alive at the time of the Crucifixion. However, what she describes here is consistent with accounts in the Gospels, which speak of earthquakes, darkness, and the dead coming out of their graves at the time of Christ's death.
>
> According to Colossians 1:17, in Christ all things consist (the Greek word used here meant literally "to cohere, to be held together"). If Christ is the force that holds together the universe's subatomic particles, then His death must have sent a terrible shiver through all reality.

I saw now a portion of our Lady Mary's compassion, for she and Christ were so joined in love that the measure of her love was also the measure of her pain. For in this showing I saw the substance of natural love, strengthened by grace, that Creation has for its Creator. The capacity of human love was fully demonstrated in Christ's mother; she loved Him more than anyone else did, and thus her sorrow and pain at His death was deeper than any other's. But *all* His followers—all His true lovers—suffered more at His death than they did at their own. If my own feelings are any indication, the least of those who followed Him loved Him so much more than themselves that their love is beyond my ability to express.

In this I saw that Christ and we are merged into one, for when He was in pain, we were in pain. All Creation that was capable of sensation suffered with Him, including the animal world. At the time of Christ's death, the very sky and earth lacked stability because of the sorrow that filled all Creation. All creatures know in their own way that Christ is their God, the One who makes them strong in what they are. When the life flowed from Jesus, all Creation was shaken. As much as it was capable, it felt the sorrow of His pain.

No wonder then that His friends suffered such pain. Even those who did not know Him, the rest of all humanity, suffered in some way. If not for the mighty, secret hand of God maintaining all life, human beings would have been destroyed.

At the time of Christ's death, two types of folk did not know Him, and these are represented by two individuals: Pilate and Saint Dennis of France. According to Saint Dennis, at the time of the Crucifixion he saw strange sorrows, peculiar happenings that filled him with great dread. He said to himself, "Either the world is ending—or the One who made all things is suffering in some mighty way." He wrote on an altar: THIS IS THE ALTAR OF THE UNKNOWN GOD. The God who out of sheer goodness makes the planets spin and gives the elements their essence, the One who provides for all humanity, good and bad, had withdrawn. No wonder then that human beings everywhere sensed the sorrow that pervaded all Creation.

In this way our Protector Jesus was brought down to nothingness, and we with Him experience nothingness as well. We will continue to share this experience until we reach His utter joy and light. (I will write more on this later.)

XIX
Jesus Is My Heaven

In this chapter, Julian speaks of the inner and outer selves. I've used the word "ego" because it is the modern term for our understanding of who we are, our external and internal identity structure, the "I" Freud wrote about in his theory of psychology. Julian explains that this "I" with which we are best acquainted has a certain reality, but all the while, beyond it exists a deeper, truer self (one which Freud never studied). As Quaker author Parker J. Palmer writes, "There is a great gulf between the way my ego wants to identify me, with its protective masks and self-serving fictions, and my true self." Julian offers us comfort in our dichotomy: the peace of this deepest inner self, she affirms, can continue undisturbed even when the ego is caught up in turmoil and despair. What Julian suggests here indicates we should be more patient with our egos, tolerating their fickle feelings and trivial selfishness, while trusting God will one day unite them with our truest selves.

Julian's focus on the "space between the Cross and Heaven" calls to my mind the Jungian concept of liminal space, the place where we get ready to move across the limits of what we were into what we are to be, a place of potential and transformation where the old boundaries that have defined our lives dissolve. The Jungian analyst Ann Belford Ulanov speaks of this space between our bodies (symbolized

> by the Cross) and our eternal spirits (symbolized by Heaven) as a place where "even our illnesses make a bridge to the transcendent."
>
> Julian also speaks of a "friendly voice" that suggested she could cross this space simply through looking at the Creator, without entering it through the vehicle of Christ's death (the word "friendly" implying that this suggestion was not dangerous or malevolent). Julian, however, chooses Christ. She accepts the pain of the Incarnation rather than seeking an alternative approach to God.

During all this, I would have looked away from the Cross, but I didn't dare. I was well aware that so long as I kept my eyes fixed on the Cross, I was absolutely safe, and I did not want to give permission for my soul to be endangered—for away from the Cross nothing was safe or certain because of the terror of the fiends.

Then a friendly voice seemed to make a suggestion: "You can look away from the Cross if you look up to Heaven to the Creator." I realized then that there was nothing dangerous in the space between the Cross and Heaven. I needed to either obey and look up, or at the very least I needed to answer the friendly suggestion. So, within my mind, I answered with all the strength of my soul: "No, I will not look away from the Cross, for You are my Heaven." I said this because I would have rather been in pain until the end of time than come to Heaven by some other means than Christ. I was fully aware that He who had bound me with pain would unbind me whenever He wanted. I chose Jesus to be my Heaven, even though at that moment I saw in Him only pain. I wanted no other Heaven but He who will be all my joy when I come there.

Since that day, I have always comforted myself with the knowledge that by Christ's grace, I chose Him to be my Heaven even in this time of such agony and sorrow. I learned then that I could make this choice always, for the rest of my life: to choose Jesus to be my Heaven in both happiness and misery.

Earlier, I had said that if I had known the degree of pain Christ experienced, I would never have prayed to share His Endurance—but I realized now that these feelings of regret were merely a natural, human reaction I experienced without my soul's permission. God did not blame me for being human and prone to weakness. A person can regret the pain of an experience at the same moment that she fully accepts it with all the power of her will. This paradox—two opposite feelings at one and the same time—is merely the expression of two aspects of our nature, the one our external ego and the other our inner spirit. The ego is mortal; it experiences pain and sorrow, and that is just the way things will always be in this life. The pain I was feeling during this time was that external aspect of my self, and that was the part that regretted ever asking to experience such agony. Meanwhile, though, the inner aspect of my self continued its life of joy, peace, and love, high above the pain and turmoil of the ego. This is the "me" that with strong and steadfast wisdom always chooses Jesus to be my Heaven.

Through this experience I learned the reality of selfhood: the inner spirit can be mistress of the ego. The ego does not disappear, of course, but the spirit need not pay much attention to its complaints. Instead, the spirit's will is fixed on becoming one with our Protector Jesus. I can only say what I saw—and I saw that the ego does not direct the spirit, but the spirit is capable of directing the ego. In the end (I saw), both our outer and inner selves will be united in joy by the grace and strength of Christ.

XX
In Love, Christ Bore Each of Our Sorrows

In her original, Julian wrote that the "Godhead" (what we might call "God-ness, the condition of being God," for which I have used "the Divine Essence") is "high and noble." We think of the word noble as having to do with a lofty moral character, but for Julian, the word still carried in it both the meaning "illustrious" and the echo of Old English roots that meant "well-known, knowable." The picture that emerges is of a light lifted up where all can see and know it.

As I said in the introduction, I'm using the word "Endurance" for Christ's experience on the Cross. The Middle English word "passion" (which Julian used in her original writing) had the same root meaning as patience; it had to do with waiting out pain. We sometimes look at pain as a "thing," an experience with a precise substance, but Julian's words here indicate that pain is something temporary, fleeting, a stream that will flow past us if we wait it out. The word "pain," which Julian used in her original, had itself a slightly different connotation in the fourteenth century: it was connected to the words "penalty" and "payment." The implication here is that pain is time's penalty, the payment exacted on all of us stuck for now in time's flow—

IN LOVE, CHRIST BORE EACH OF OUR SORROWS

> but that once we are beyond time, pain will have no reality. By becoming incarnate, the Divine entered time; according to Julian, Christ then carried his pain with him into Heaven, a treasured memento of his Incarnation, where he transformed the meaning of pain for us all.

Our Protector's pain went on and on. His union with Divinity gave His humanity strength to suffer more than an ordinary human could. What's more, the sum of His suffering was more than all human pain from the beginning to the end of human history. He who is the highest and worthiest was also the One who was most totally despised, most utterly negated by our separation from God.

This knowledge of Christ's pain is the pinnacle of His Endurance. In this showing He brought to my mind the way in which the glory of the Divine Essence, the way in which it is lifted up high for all to see and experience, is at the same time united with the particular vulnerability of a human body. I also realized how much humans hate the experience of pain; and yet He who was most fully human, most totally whole, most full of love, was also the One who had the most strength and resources for enduring pain.

He suffered the separation from God of each and every human soul; He knew each individual's sorrow and desolation, and with the love and closeness of a family member, He shared each human pain. (For just as our Lady shared her Child's pain, so He experienced hers at an even deeper level.) All during the time He was capable of experiencing human sensations, He suffered and sorrowed for us. And now He is risen, and His body is no longer like ours—and yet still He suffers for us.

As I watched all this—a gift of His generosity—I saw that the love He has for our souls is so great and strong that He chose His pain willingly, eagerly even; He felt no rebellion, no resentment, no harshness.

If, touched by Divine grace, you can catch a glimpse of this, you shall see the truth of Christ's suffering: a suffering that endures all the cost of being human—a painful price that will be transformed into everlasting, overwhelming joy by the strength of Christ's endurance.

XXI
Temporary Pain Yields Endless Knowledge

> Julian describes in greater depth in this chapter the release from pain that happens at the moment of our deaths (when we are also released from time). Her image of death is a comforting one of laughter and gladness. She acknowledges that earthly sorrow is real, and all the more meaningful because Christ shared it to its utmost depths—and yet she also affirms that this world's suffering is a temporary thing unable to survive outside time. Once Eternity touches our pains, they will disappear like soap bubbles.

It is God's will (as I understand it) that we perceive Christ's Endurance in more than one way. First, that we regard the cruel pain He suffered with sorrow and compassion. Our Protector showed me this during my time of revelation, giving me both the strength and the grace to understand.

But the second perception of Christ's Endurance happened as I watched Him hanging on the Cross, struggling to see the moment when His spirit left Him, thinking I would then see His dead body—but I never saw this. At the very moment I thought His life could last no longer and that His actual death would be revealed to me, my gaze never shifted, and yet His face changed suddenly, even as I watched. The change in His expression changed me as well, and all at once I was as glad and happy as could be. I seemed to hear our Protector say in my mind, with laughter in His voice, "What happened to all your pain and grief?" and my mind filled with amusement.

I understood what our Protector meant. If we willingly unite ourselves with His Endurance and pain, staying with Him, by His grace and help, until the ultimate moment of His life—then we will experience what He did: the sudden transformation at death of earthly pain to Heaven's joy. There is no passage of time between the one and the other, and then everything is turned into joy. That is why He asked in this showing, "What happened to all your pain and grief?" For Earth's arrows will lose their points in Heaven; they will no longer have the power to pierce and wound, and we shall be made whole, filled up with blessing.

I realized then that if Christ were to show us now the joy of His face, then no pain of Earth (or anywhere else) would bother us, for we would know only delight and happiness. But instead, He shows us the time of His Endurance, as He experienced it during His time on Earth, and we too, trapped by the demands of our frail bodies, are in distress and torment. He allows us this experience because He knows that it will lift us higher with Him in His ultimate bliss and joy. In exchange for this little pain that we experience here, we shall have a high and endless knowledge of God such as we could never have had otherwise. The more severe our distress here (as we endure with Him the Cross), the greater will be our splendor when we are with Him in His Kingdom.

The Ninth Revelation

XXII
Love That Is Greater Than All Pain

> The concepts Julian describes in this chapter may seem difficult, but what is clear is the immensity of Christ's love for us.

Our good Protector said then, "Are you pleased that I suffered for you?"

I answered, "Yes, good Protector, I thank You. Yes, good Protector, blessed may You be."

Then Jesus, our kind Protector, said, "If you are pleased, then I am pleased. It is My delight, My joy, an endless satisfaction, that I endured for you—and if I could endure still more, I would."

At this point, my awareness was lifted up into Heaven, and I saw there three heavens (three homes where God resides), a sight that filled me with wonder. But although I saw three heavens—all contained in the blessed humanity of Christ—none was more than the other, none less, none higher, none lower. They were equal in joy.

Christ revealed to me the first heaven: the Creator. I don't mean to say I perceived a physical likeness of the Creator but rather the Divine Essence and Action. I saw that the Creator is in Christ, and the Divine Action bestows a reward to the Christ Child. This gift gives Jesus so much joy that no other reward could have pleased Him more. This first heaven is the Creator's pleasure, the Divine Satisfaction with all that Jesus has done to save and heal us.

In this sense, Christ did not only purchase us with His death but we are also the heartfelt gift of the Creator to the Child. We are Christ's joy, we are His reward, we are His worth, and we are His crown. (How amazing and delightful that we are His crown!) We give Jesus such joy that He completely disregards the torment and humiliation He endured as He died on the Cross. This is the second heaven.

When He said, "If I could endure still more, I would," I realized that Jesus would die over and over if He could; His love would never let Him rest so long as His death had power to help me. I looked carefully at this portion of the vision, trying to count how many times Jesus would die for me if I needed Him, and the number was beyond my ability to count or comprehend. And yet no matter how many times He died, He would simply disregard it yet again, for His pain seems to Him like a mere trifle in comparison with His love.

If Christ's human flesh suffered only once, at a particular point in time, His goodness is nevertheless offered continually, endlessly; His love is always ready to give Himself for me. If He had told me He would make a new Heaven and a new Earth because of His love for me, that would not mean so much as His willingness to give His life countless times. For me, this is the greatest offering our Protector God could make to the human soul.

He was saying to me: "Why wouldn't I also do for you those things that cause Me no pain, since I would willingly suffer and die for you again and again?" I realized then that His love is as much greater than His pain as Heaven is greater than Earth. His agony on the Cross draws our attention, for it was a worthy thing, achieved at a particular point in time by means of His love. But His love knows no time; it is without beginning and end. That is why He said, "If I could endure still more, I would." He didn't say, "If you needed me to suffer more, I would"; no, if He could, He would, whether I needed Him to or not.

All this—Christ's work and our reunion with God—was laid out and ordered by the Divine Spirit at work (the third heaven). In this I saw Christ's joy. I knew His delight would have been incomplete if He had left any part of it undone.

XXIII
The Glad Giver

> Here Julian emphasizes the reality of Divine joy, a joy that is the fulfillment of love.

I saw revealed three heavens in Christ's words: "It is My delight, My joy, an endless satisfaction." The delight I understood to be the Creator's pleasure; the joy was the Child's wealth; and the endless satisfaction was the Spirit's work. The Creator is pleased, the Child's worth is acknowledged, and the Spirit is satisfied.

In my visions, our kind Protector showed His Endurance to me in five separate ways: the first was the blood that fell from His head; the second was the discoloration of His face; the third was the bleeding of His body; the fourth was His dying. I have already described these pains that He endured. The fifth was the joy and delight of His Endurance.

For it is God's will that we enjoy our safety and wholeness (rather than experience this life with sorrow and heaviness), and that is why God wants us to be comforted and strengthened, and yes, even laugh, as our souls are occupied by grace. For we are God's joy; in us, God has endless delight; and by God's grace, we shall experience the same happiness.

THE GLAD GIVER

All that God has done for us, is doing for us, and ever shall do for us cost nothing; the Incarnation cost only the Divine Essence, beginning with Christ's birth and lasting through His rising on Easter morning. This measure of time is the load Christ carried, the sacrifice He made, the cost He paid for our redemption—and this is the act that gives Him endless joy, as I have already described.

Jesus wants us to pay attention to the joy that is in the Trinity as a result of our reunion with God, and He desires that we experience this joy equally. In other words, we should have the same joy Christ has as much as we are able.

The entire Trinity was at work during Christ's Endurance, ministering abundant strength and grace to us through Him—but only the young woman's Child, the human being, suffered. And because of His Endurance, all the Trinity has endless joy. I understood all this from Christ's words, "Are you pleased? . . . If you are pleased, then I am pleased." It was as if He said, "Your pleasure is all the satisfaction I need. I ask no other reward for the torment I endured than that you be happy."

Christ is a glad giver. A glad giver pays little attention to the gift he gives; all his attention is on the pleasure and happiness of the one to whom he gives. If the receiver is grateful and happy, then the giver disregards any cost or effort that went into the gift, for he is only aware of the delight that the loved one's joy gives him.

All this was shown to me clearly, with a sense of fullness and completion. I also want to call attention to Christ's use of the word "endless." I understood that this meant that He was both endlessly glad—and that we had been rescued from the endless pain of separation from God.

The Tenth Revelation

XXIV
The Wounds of Love

> We may be put off by Julian's description of looking into Christ's wound, like the special effects on a forensic TV show where the viewer is suddenly inside a body, seeing events at the cellular level. But the only message that really matters in this chapter is this: we can laugh with joy, even in the midst of life's challenges, because God loves us.

With a glad face, our Protector looked down at His side then and laughed. I seemed to follow His gaze, so that I actually entered the wound in His flesh. I found there a beautiful and delightful place, large enough for all humanity to rest in peace and love—a long, wide space of endless joy enclosed within Him. I thought then of His blood that He shed for us, and I seemed to see His heart as though it were split in two.

This vision inspired me to think about the endless love of the Divine Essence, a love that is without beginning, that continues on at this moment, and shall exist forevermore. I heard our Protector say, His voice full of joy, "Look how much I loved you."

I felt as if He had said, "My darling, look and see your Protector, your God who is your Maker and your endless joy, see what satisfaction and delight I take in your safety and wholeness. Rejoice, My love, with Me."

And in case that wasn't enough to make me understand, I heard Him say, "Look! See how much I loved you. See—I loved you so much before I died for you that I was willing to die for you—and now I *have* died for you and suffered willingly on your behalf. All My bitter pain and cruel torment has been turned to endless joy and delight, both for Me and for you. So after all that, why would you think that if you pray for what pleases Me, I wouldn't leap to joyfully grant your prayer? For you are made whole by pleasing Me, and you find your endless joy and delight with Me."

As simply as I can say it, this is the message of this showing: "Look how much I loved you." Our good Protector showed me this to make us glad, to make us laugh for joy.

The Eleventh Revelation

XXV
In Mary, We Know We Are Loved

> In this chapter, Julian shows us Christ's love for his human mother, a love embedded in the very meaning of the Incarnation, and one in which, says Julian, we too can be pleased and comforted. The image of the Divine that Julian describes throughout her book is not abstract or beyond human contact; instead, the God she portrays is deeply personal and intimate, a God who delights in individual relationships even as Divine love flows through all reality.

With the same look of joy and laughter, our Protector looked down to the right, reminding me that this was where our Lady stood during her Child's Endurance. He said to me, "Do you want to see her?" It was as if with these words He were saying, "I know full well that you want to see My mother, because after Myself, she is the greatest joy I can show you. She gives me pleasure and honor, and all creation longs to see her."

Because the love He has for her is so unique, so high and amazing, He showed me our Lady in the midst of a great joy, as though

He were saying to me, "As you see how I love her, you too will take joy in the love I have for her and she for Me." At the same time, our Protector was speaking to all human beings, as if they were a single person, saying, "See in her how much you too are loved. It was love for you that caused Me to raise her so high. She makes me happy, and I want her to make you happy as well."

After Christ Himself, Mary is the most joyful sight. But this showing was not intended to make me expect to see her physical presence in this life; instead, I am meant to perceive the strength of her goodness, her integrity, her wisdom, and her love, and that by their light, I might better know myself and be filled with reverent awe for my God.

So when our Protector said, "Do you want to see her?" I answered, "Yes, good Protector, thank You. Yes, good Protector, if this be Your will." I prayed this many times, thinking I would see her physical presence, but I did not. Instead, Jesus gave me a spiritual vision of her. Where before I had seen her as small and simple, now He showed her to me as someone high, lifted up, and splendid, more pleasing to Him than all Creation.

He wants us to understand that as we take joy in Him, we should also take joy in her, and in the delight He has in her and she in Him. To help me understand better, He gave me this example: If a person loved a creature more than any other, wouldn't she want all creatures to love and delight in the creature she loved so greatly?

When Jesus said, "Do you want to see her?" I thought He couldn't have said anything that could have made me happier. With this spiritual vision, He showed me nothing besides our Lady Mary as she stood filled with delight, reverence, and joy.

The Twelfth Revelation

XXVI
"It Is I"

In this chapter, words finally fail Julian. Despite years of pondering the meaning of each aspect of her showings, she still cannot express the deepest essence of this moment of her vision.

After this our Protector showed Himself in all His splendor, more so than I had yet seen Him in these showings. From this I learned that our souls will never be at rest until they come to Him in the knowledge that He is the fullness of joy, intimate and welcoming, full of delight and the very essence of life.

Our Protector Jesus then said over and over, "It is I, I am the One: I am the One who is highest, I am the One you love, I am all that you enjoy, I am what you serve, I am that which you long for most, I am all that you desire, I am who lives in your thoughts, I am everything. It is I the Church teaches to you, and it is I who have shown Myself to you here." He said this so many times that the words were too many for me to grasp; they were beyond my strength to comprehend. These words are the best and highest, in my opinion, for in them, they contain . . .

I cannot express what they contain! Words fail me, but the joy this showing gave me was beyond anything the intellect could wish for or the soul desire. I cannot write here what this meant to me. You who read this, may God give you grace to love and understand our Protector's meaning.

The Thirteenth Revelation

XXVII
All Shall Be Well

Julian struggles here with the age-old problem of pain. (How can a loving God allow pain and suffering?) She once again expresses her conviction that "sin has no substance, no being." Compare her words to what Saint Augustine wrote in the fifth century:

> All things that exist, therefore, seeing that the Creator of them all is supremely good, are themselves good. But because they are not like their Creator, supremely and unchangeably good, their good may be diminished and increased. But for good to be diminished is an evil, although, however much it may be diminished, it is necessary, if the being is to continue, that some good should remain to constitute the being. For however small or of whatever kind the being may be, the good which makes it a being cannot be destroyed without destroying the being itself. . . . So long as a being is in the process of corruption, there is in it some good of which it is being deprived; and if a part of the being should remain which cannot be corrupted, this will certainly be an incorruptible being, and accordingly the process of corruption will result in the manifestation of this great good. . . . Every being, therefore, is a good. . . .

Plato (the Greek philosopher who lived in the fifth century before Christ) and Thomas Aquinas (the

> thirteenth-century theologian and philosopher) also shared similar views of evil as non-being. They saw God as all perfection and complete Being; below God lay a continuum that began with things that were "more real" and closer to God and ended at the other end with evil and non-being. Evil was thus an absence of good and was in effect an illusion.
>
> But Julian goes even further in this chapter and says that sin was unavoidable, a statement that may seem radical, if not heretical. Her conclusion to this line of thought is probably her most famous statement: despite the fact that no one has yet totally found an answer to the problem of pain—evil may be ultimately unreal but it is still a part of our human experience—"All shall be well, and all shall be well, and absolutely everything shall be well."

Next the Protector brought to my mind the longing I had always had for Him. I saw then that nothing had been in my way but sin. As I thought about humanity in general, I couldn't help but think, "If sin had not been made, we would have all been clean, like the Protector, just as He made us."

In my confusion, I always wondered why God's great and wise foreknowledge had not prevented sin's beginning. If He had, I thought, all would have been well. I had given up thinking like this, and yet I still sorrowed over the separation that had arisen between human beings and God.

But Jesus—who was showing me all I needed to know—answered these thoughts now and said, "Sin was unavoidable. But all shall be well, and all shall be well, and absolutely everything shall be well."

In this stark, unadorned word—sin—our Protector brought to my mind all that is not good: the malice and total negation of all He was, the pain He bore for us in this life; His death, and all the spiritual and physical pain and suffering of His creatures. (For we are all partially negated—our full and real identities are being destroyed—and we shall be even more negated as we follow Jesus, until we are made totally whole, completely pure, with all death washed away from our bodies and all that is selfish purged from our inner selves.) As I watched this vision unfold, I saw all the pain that had ever been or ever would be, and I understood that Christ's Endurance was the worst pain of all.

All this was showed to me in no more than a touch and then it was quickly passed over. Our good Protector did not want us to be terrified by this; He wants our comfort. But through it all, I saw no sin, for I believe sin has no substance, no being. In effect, it does not exist, for it can only be known through the pain it causes. This pain, as I understand it, is something that purifies us, that teaches us about ourselves, and that makes us rely on God's mercy. But our Protector's Endurance is meant to comfort us in the midst of this pain; that is what He wants.

Because our good Protector loves us so tenderly, He is quick to comfort, saying, "Granted, sin has caused you all this pain, but all shall be well, and all shall be well, and absolutely everything shall be well." These words were said with so much love, with no hint of blame. So if God does not blame me for my sin, I would be rude to blame Him for it! We are a family, connected by intimate bonds, and guilt and blame have no part in such a relationship.

In these words I saw a marvelous and lofty mystery that is hid in God, a mystery that will be laid out for us to see in Heaven. Then we will know the true reason why God allowed sin to come into the world, and the sight will fill us with endless joy.

XXVIII
Christ Lives in Our Love for Each Other

> Julian here refuses to accept the common Christian belief that God looks with hatred and horror at our sin. If we can feel compassion and mercy for others, she insists, how much more does Christ? In fact, she says, human compassion is actually Christ living in us.

I saw through all this that Christ has compassion for us because of sin. And just as in the earlier showing where I experienced a portion of Christ's pain, now I also experienced a portion of His compassion for my fellow Christ-followers, those well-loved people who will be kept safe forever. For God's servants, the Holy Church, shall be shaken by the world's sorrow and anguish and trials, the way you might shake a rug in the wind.

The Protector answered my pity with this: "In Heaven's endless worth-giving and everlasting joy, I will comfort all sorrow." As contradictory as this may seem, I saw that our Protector takes joy in His servants' troubles even as He feels both compassion and sorrow. In the lives of all whom He loves, He allows some trouble to enter. These trials are not punishments; in His eyes they have no shame, even though others may regard them with scorn, mockery, and rejection. When we are abused and violated, snatched out of our sense of who we are, we are at the same time rescued from this life's emptiness, and our path toward Heaven then lies more clearly before us. There we will experience endless delight. For He said to me: "I will smash your empty desires and your unhealthy selfishness—and after that, I will gather you together, completely clean, completely whole, with all your hardness and rigidity melted and softened, made one with Me."

I realized then that the compassion we feel for each other is actually Christ in us. He showed me again here the same laying down of His identity He demonstrated in His Endurance. He longs for us to feel joy—and to be comforted from our pain. His desire is for us to understand that all our troubles will be turned to worth and profit through His Endurance; He wants us to see that we are not alone in our suffering, but that He is with us. He is the soil where the roots of our lives are nourished; He is the foundation that keeps our lives firm and solid. What He suffered for us—the loss of His very identity as God's Son—is so far greater than any pain we will ever experience that we will never even comprehend it.

If we focus on these thoughts it will help us not to complain and become discouraged in the midst of life's difficulties. When we consider the ways we have separated ourselves from God, it is no wonder we encounter troubles—and yet Divine love makes excuses for us, and in Christ's generosity, He removes all blame from us. Instead, with mercy and compassion, God sees us as though we were children, completely innocent, with nothing whatsoever unlovable about us.

XXIX
Sin's Harm

> Julian continues to struggle with the problem of evil—and again affirms God's creative power to mend all that is broken.

And yet as I looked at all these things, I was troubled and sad. In my mind, I said to our Protector, as respectfully as I could, "Ah, good Protector! How can all be well, when our separation from You has damaged Creation so terribly?" I was hoping Christ would explain all this to me more openly and clearly, so that my sense of worry and sorrow would be eased.

Our Protector answered patiently, with an expression of love on His face, showing me that Adam's separation from God was the worst harm that ever came to the world and ever will, till the end of time. This is the insight the Holy Church knows and teaches throughout the Earth. However, Christ taught me to focus my attention instead on the bright and splendid fulfillment of all life—for this mending of what was broken is more pleasing to God and of infinitely more worth than Adam's sin was harmful. Our Protector wants us to pay attention to this thought: "If I have made well this most basic damage to reality, this separation that is the worst that has ever befallen Creation, then you can rest assured I will also be able to make well all other things."

XXX
Truth Revealed, Truth Hidden

> Julian indicates that even though God has revealed a portion of Divine truth to humanity, there is another piece that has not been revealed, that we cannot even imagine. As the Apostle Paul wrote in 1 Corinthians, "No eye has seen, no ear has heard, and no mind has imagined what God has prepared for those who love him" (2:9 NLT).

Christ next made me think about His truth's two sides. The one aspect is our Rescuer and our safety and wholeness, and this part is revealed to us openly, clearly, with plenty of light for us to see. All humanity who have good intentions—or who will come to have them—can see this. This is the reality that connects us to God, and this is what draws our spirits and teaches our minds, internally by the Holy Spirit and externally by the Church. Our Protector wants us to busy our thoughts with this aspect of truth, enjoying Him even as He enjoys us. The more fully we partake of this reality, with reverence and humility, the more He will thank us and the more enriched we will be as we enjoy our Protector.

But beyond this aspect of truth that He has revealed to us, all is hidden from our view. This is our God's secret. Just as a nation's leader may keep some of his thoughts and actions hidden from the citizens of the land, so God does not reveal everything to us. This is the role of the leader; our role as citizens is to respect the leader's wisdom, and trust that he knows what he is doing even when we do not understand. Some people worry and fret over truth's hidden side, and our Protector has compassion for their anxiety. But we would be happier—and we would make God happy—if we could simply trust what we don't know to Him. The saints in Heaven desire to know only what our Protector shows them, and we should discipline ourselves to be like them. Then all our desires will be within the Protector's will, and we will be like them, for in God's sight, we are all united into One.

And in this showing I was taught that as we trust and enjoy our Rescuer, Jesus, we shall have everything in Him.

XXXI
Christ Thirsts for Our Well-Being

Earlier (in chapter X), Julian affirmed that seeking and finding, longing and fulfillment are the two-sided coin of normal human experience. Here, she carries this thought further and explains that it is actually Divine longing and fulfillment we experience, for just as we thirst for the Divine, Christ also thirsts for our completion in God. It is his longing that flows through our lives, pulling us toward God.

In this chapter we have again used the word "good," relying on the Middle German word for "unite," which is much closer to the word Julian used than our modern word "goodness." The still-older Sanskrit word from which the Middle German evolved carried the meaning of "that which one clings to." We have done our best to retain the nuances of these meanings that would have shaded Julian's fourteenth-century language.

In this way, our Protector answered my questions and doubts, comforting me with these words: "I may make everything well, I can make everything well, I will make everything well, and I shall make everything well. You shall see for yourself that absolutely everything shall be well!"

When He said, "I may," I understood He was referring to the Father; when He said, "I can," He was speaking of the Child; when He said, "I will," He meant the Holy Spirit; and when He said, "I shall," I assumed He was speaking of the Blessed Trinity, three Persons and one Truth. Then when He said, "You shall see for yourself," I understood that He meant all humanity united into One as they are rescued and made safe by the blessed Trinity. God wants us to take refuge within the walls of these five phrases; enclosed by them, we find rest and peace.

And once we have, Christ's thirst will be satisfied. For this is His longing, a yearning of endless love that will endure until we who have been rescued and made safe, and all who will be, are united with Him, made whole in His joy. In this life, we are not yet as completely whole and healed as we shall be on that day.

We know this by faith, but it is the same truth that all my visions showed me as well: that Christ Jesus is both Divine and human. The Divine Essence is highest bliss without beginning or end, a joy that can neither be increased nor decreased for it is constant and unchanging. This was revealed clearly in every showing, especially the twelfth, when the Divine Voice said, "I am that which is highest." Through faith, we believe in Christ's humanity; with the strength of the Divine Essence working through His humanity, He was able to endure pain and death, so that we could share His joy. This was the purpose of His humanity, and in the ninth revelation, He said to me, "My Endurance on your behalf is a joy and a delight and an endless pleasure." This is the joy of His work, and this is what He meant when He said in that same showing that we are His joy, we are His reward, we are His worth, and we are His crown.

Christ is the intelligence that works in our spirits with limitless brightness, but His Body, in which all of us are knit together, is not yet complete in its light and life. That is why He had always experienced, without beginning or end, the same longing and thirst He experienced when He hung from the Cross, and He will continue to thirst until the last human being has been rescued and entered into His joy.

Just as certainly as compassion and mercy describe the Divine Essence, so do thirst and longing. (By the strength and goodness of Christ's longing we are drawn to Him. Our own souls answer His with yearning; without this, none of us would come to Heaven.) The Divine thirst and longing rises out of endless Unity, that which we all cling to, in the same way that compassion and mercy also spring from this eternal Unity, the magnet that draws our souls. For even though longing and compassion are two different qualities, from my perspective, they are drawn together into a single point: the Divine yearning that will endure as long as we are in need, a yearning that draws us upward into joy, never ceasing until the end of time when we are finally made one.

And so Divine mercy and longing endure, for at the same time, God's wisdom and love know the best time for the end to come.

XXXII
The Great Deed That Heals All Deeds

> Julian asserts a paradox here: that Hell and eternal damnation are true (as taught by the Church) AND that everything shall ultimately be "well." Somehow, through a still-unknown creative act, writes Julian, God will totally heal all that sin has broken. The paradox Julian describes is reminiscent of some of the paradoxes found in quantum physics: for instance, light is both a particle and a wave, depending on your point of view. The two realities are both real, both true—and the Divine Power that made everything out of nothing, Julian affirms, can also fulfill what seem to be two contradictory perspectives.

At one point our Protector had said, "Everything shall be well," and another time He said, "You shall see for yourself that absolutely everything shall be well." From these two statements, I drew different meanings.

First, I believe Christ wants us to know He not only pays attention to high and great things, things that are obvious and important, but also, equally, to small things that seem trivial, simple,

THE GREAT DEED THAT HEALS ALL DEEDS

and hidden. This is what He meant when He said, "*absolutely everything* shall be well." He wants us to understand that not even the least thing will be forgotten.

But I also understood from these phrases that although some deeds appear so evil from our perspective, so hurtful and damaging that no good could possibly come from them, God does not see as we do. We look at the world's events with such sorrow and grief that our vision is clouded, and we cannot see joy. But we are thinking with human reason, a perspective that is still so limited, blind, and simple that we cannot comprehend the joyful Trinity's amazing wisdom, strength, and unity.

When Jesus said, "*You shall see for yourself* that absolutely everything shall be well," it was as though He were saying, "Look now with the eyes of faith and trust, for one day you will actually see—and in that day your joy will be complete."

In these same words, I understand the strength and comfort we can find in the Divine works that have not yet come to be. I believe on the Last Day, the blessed Trinity shall accomplish an amazing deed. We will never know what that deed is until it has been accomplished.

Divine goodness and love wants us to know that this deed will take place, while Divine strength and wisdom hides from us what it will be and how it will be done. God wants us to know it will take place, so that our minds will be eased and our love will be made stable by peace, so that we can stop worrying about the troublesome things that hold us back from truly enjoying the Divine. This Great Deed was planned out from the beginning and hidden within the Divine Essence, and by it shall absolutely everything be made well.

For just as the joyful Trinity made everything out of nothing, so the same Trinity can make well all that is not well.

ALL SHALL BE WELL

As I realized all this, I was full of amazement and confusion. I thought, "Our faith's foundation is in the Bible, and we believe that the Bible's truth shall never be lost. Part of our faith has always been that many creatures will be condemned because of their separation from God: the angels whose pride made them fall from Heaven; human beings who have never heard the gospel; and also humans who have heard the gospel and rejected it in their lives. The Church teaches that all these shall be eternally condemned to Hell—so how can it be possible that everything will be well?" The revelation Jesus showed me seemed to contradict what I had always been taught.

The only answer I received was this: "That which is impossible for you is not impossible for Me. I will keep My word in all things, and I will make absolutely everything well." And so I learned to believe these two seemingly contradictory truths, holding them both in my mind at the same time. I resolved to continue within the Church's teachings while I also believed that in the end, absolutely everything will be well, just as our Protector had showed me.

This is the Great Deed our Protector shall do; in this deed, He will keep the Divine Word revealed in Scripture but at the same time, He will make absolutely everything well. How Christ can do this no one knows, and no one will ever know until it has been accomplished.

XXXIII
Blind Faith Balanced with Mental Focus

> The conclusions Julian reaches here about Hell are similar to what C. S. Lewis described in his book *The Great Divorce*, where those who have rejected God "simply cease to exist." Julian is careful to say, however, that this is her own conclusion, rather than a part of the revelations she received.
>
> In this chapter we see again the care Julian takes to tiptoe around any possibility that the Church might find her guilty of heresy. Her conclusion, however, is a practical one: the more we theorize intellectually about the mysterious workings of Divine reality, the further we are from experiencing that reality for ourselves.

Despite all I had learned, I was curious about Hell and Purgatory, and as much as I dared, I wanted to see what they looked like. I'm not saying that I needed proof that the Church's teachings are correct, for I steadfastly believe in the Church, but I felt that if I could understand all aspects of my faith more clearly, my life would be worth more, both to God and to myself.

But despite my curiosity, I could see nothing beyond what I had seen during the first showing, when I saw that God has reproved and eternally condemned the devil. I understood from this that all who are like the devil, whether they call themselves "Christians" or not, shall simply cease to exist in the eyes of God and all the Divine Holy Ones.

This is my own conclusion, which I drew from the fact that the revelations I received focused only on goodness, with little mention of evil—and at the same time, I could not believe that anything in these showings was intended to make me reject the Church's teachings.

I saw the Endurance of Christ in various revelations—the first, the second, the fifth, and the eighth—and I shared the sorrow of our Lady and Christ's friends when they saw Him in such agony. But during those showings of the Cross, I never saw anything about the human beings who put Him to death. My faith teaches me that they were eternally condemned and cursed (unless they turned to God through Divine grace). And I believe I must keep my beliefs and ideas within the Church's boundary lines; it is my desire and prayer to stay safe within my faith to the end of my life.

This is how I understand God's will: that we focus our minds on the way the Divine works in the world around us, trusting that we shall one day see the Great Deed that will right all wrongs. Let us be like our brothers and sisters who are saints in Heaven, whose only desire is to see—or not see—whatever Divine Love reveals to them.

I saw that the true essence of our Protector's teaching is this: the more we are preoccupied with sacred secrets, the Divine mysteries, the further we are from experiencing them.

XXXIV
God Reveals All We Need to Know

After struggling again with the problem of sin and Hell, Julian reaffirms that we are to simply trust God that all things shall be made well.

The Divine Protector showed me two kinds of secret things. First, is the Great Secret with all its details, which is hidden from us until the time when it shall be revealed. But there are other secrets God wants to show us. These are secrets not because God has hidden them from us, but because our own blindness and ignorance obscure our vision. Because of this, God feels compassion and sorrow for us; Divine mercy longs to reveal these secrets to us so we can love and cling to God more wholly. All that is helpful to us will be shown to us. That is why these showings were given to me, and that is why the Church's teachings are passed on to us.

God is delighted with all those who humbly struggle to accept the Church's teachings. God is the Ground and the Essence, the Teaching and the Teacher, the End and the Reward for each loving soul who labors here in this life.

This is made known to all souls as the Holy Spirit makes clear. I sincerely hope that all those who seek this knowledge shall find it, for they are seeking God.

All that I have described so far, and that which I still have to tell, comforts our fears about sin. For in the third showing, when I saw that God is the Verb in every action, I saw no sin, no separation from God, and I saw that all is well. And even when Divine revelation showed me the separation that lies between God and us, still I heard this message: "All shall be well."

XXXV
Particular Attachments Hinder Us

What Julian describes in this chapter is a truth endorsed by many spiritual disciplines: attachment (whether to people, things, or our own egos) gets in the way of our experience of Divine grace and joy. Julian is not saying we should deny ourselves the pleasures of the material world (instead, she affirms God's presence in all of life), only that we should not become attached to any specific aspect of the world around us. The world changes—but God does not, and the Divine presence continues to be revealed anew.

In this chapter, we have worked to better express the original meanings of righteousness and rectitude. Like "goodness," these are words that now carry with them heavy baggage full of morality, but the original meaning was simply "straight, upright, stretched out in a line": in other words, the opposite of bent, crooked, and distorted.

Julian also uses the word "true" in this chapter, which we have kept, since our modern meaning carries within it most of the same connotations the word had for Julian. However, we tend today to define

> "true" as simply the opposite of "false," as though the negative quality draws a line around truth's shape (instead of the other way around). By contrast, Julian's word had evolved more recently from older meanings based on positive qualities: these included "firm," "strong," "faithful and reliable," and "sure." Etymologists speculate that the very oldest root word may have been "tree," with the implication that to be true means to be "steadfast as an oak." This gives the concept of being true (both to ourselves and to God) a more sense-based and dynamic meaning, one that speaks of deep roots and sturdy branches.

After God had showed me so fully and joyously the Divine goodness, I wanted to know if a particular person I loved would continue to enjoy life and grace. But in my desire for a specific revelation, I seemed to hinder myself, and I saw nothing. It was as though I heard then a friendly voice saying, "Look at the big picture rather than the small. See Divine grace as it has been shown to you in everything around you. It is worth more to God if you can perceive the Divine Presence in all life rather than merely in any specific creation."

Through this I learned that we should not allow ourselves to become attached to individual aspects of Creation, but instead, we should enjoy God's worth in everything. This means as well that we will not be greatly distressed if we lose one aspect of life, for we can rest in the confidence that the whole of reality is still fine—for absolutely everything shall be well.

PARTICULAR ATTACHMENTS HINDER US

We are most wholly joyful when we see God in all things. The same sacred strength, wisdom, and love that created the world also continue to work within all Creation, bringing each and every thing to God. In good time, we shall be able to see the reality of this. The foundation for this truth was revealed to me in the first showing, and explained more fully in the third, when I saw God revealed in a single Point.

Every Divine action is a straight, true line to God; God's tolerance for all that exists is worth much. These two statements embrace both good and evil, for all that is good comes from Divine action, and all that is evil is nevertheless allowed by God. I'm not saying that the evil itself is valuable—only that God's tolerance of it is. Divine goodness, endless and enduring, shall be revealed through Divine gentleness and humility, by the actions of mercy and grace.

Straight lines cannot be made more straight; they are without flaw. God is the essence of straightness—and each Divine action is yet another line drawn straight and true, set in place from the beginning by the heights of Divine strength, wisdom, and goodness. And just as God desires what is best for each aspect of Creation, so does the Holy Spirit lead all things straight to that goal. God makes God happy! All that God accomplishes increases Divine joy.

How sweet is the taste of this unity that lies at the heart of all things! In Heaven, all the souls who were bent and broken will be made permanently straight in God's eyes by the power of Divine goodness. We will be kept true to our real selves and to God for ever and ever. This is an amazing truth that lifts us higher than all Creation.

Mercy is an action that comes from God's goodness, and mercy will never cease to act so long as sin is allowed to separate us from God. Once nothing separates us any longer, then mercy's action can come to an end. Everything then shall be brought straight and whole, and everything shall remain that way endlessly.

God allows us to fall, but by the joy, strength, and wisdom of Divine love we are kept safe—and by mercy and grace, we are lifted up within the many facets of Divine joy. In this way, through both generous mercy and stringent straightness of heart, God wants us to endlessly see and love the Divine Presence in our lives. When we look at life from this perspective, we are filled with contentment and eternal joy.

XXXVI
Our Sin Does Not Hinder God's Goodness

> Here Julian elaborates on the security and joy we find as we trust Divine creativity to make whole all that has been broken.

Our Protector God showed me that the Deed (which shall make all things well) shall be accomplished by Divine power. Although I do nothing but sin, my sin will do nothing to stop the action of God's goodness. Contemplating this is a joy from Heaven for those souls who long with intimate expectation for God's will. The Deed begins here, in this life, and it shall give worth and wealth to God and to those who love the Divine on Earth. As we come to Heaven, we shall see it with marvelous delight, this Deed that shall continue its work until the Last Day. Its worth and joy shall endure forever in Heaven in the presence of God and all the Holy Ones.

Our Protector showed me this deed so that we would rejoice in God and in all that the Divine achieves. When I saw that this showing continued, I understood that it was revealed to me as a foretaste of what lies ahead. God showed this to me with such joy, wanting me to accept the knowledge with faith and trust, while all the while the Deed itself was kept secret from me.

Through this I understood that God does not want us to dread that which is unknown but instead to rest in love and joy. Divine love is so great that it reveals to us all that we need to know, that which enriches us and makes us grow. And even that which is kept secret is still revealed to us in guarded glimpses, so that we will trust in God's endless kindness, rejoicing in all that is revealed and in all that is hidden. If we do this with determination and humility, we shall find great comfort, and we shall receive God's endless thanks.

The Deed shall be done for me; in other words, it shall be done for all humanity. It shall be worthy, marvelous, and abundant, done by the hand of God, and seeing it will be the greatest joy that shall ever be. Humanity is bent and separated from God, but all that will have no consequence whatsoever once the Deed has been accomplished.

It was as if our Protector God said, "Look and see! Here is the substance of humility, the substance of love, the substance of your nothingness, the substance of your joy in Me. In My love, enjoy Me. Of all things, this pleases Me most."

And whenever in this life we foolishly turn our thoughts to condemnation, our Protector God touches us gently, getting our attention, calling us with joy, speaking to our souls: "Let love fill you, My dear and valuable child. Turn to Me—I am enough for you—and take joy in your Rescuer and in your safety and wholeness."

I am convinced that the soul who through grace is able to thoroughly grasp the Divine offering will see and feel that this is how our Protector works in us. Although the Deed is achieved for all humanity in general, it also encompasses each individual. But exactly what our Protector shall do for creation is still unknown to me. For there are two deeds, one that can be known in part here, and the Great Deed that cannot be known, either in Heaven or Earth, until it has been accomplished.

I also received a new understanding of how miracles work: "I have done miracles here before, many and varied, exalted and amazing, worthy and great. And as I have done in the past, so I do continually, and I shall do in time to come." Sorrow, anguish, and troubles come before miracles, so that we know our own weakness and the ill effects of our separation from God—so that we are humbled and filled with fear until we cry out for help and grace. This is the moment when miracles take place, and they come from Divine potency, wisdom, and goodness, demonstrating God's strength and the joys of Heaven as much as we are capable of understanding in this fleeting life, so that our faith, hope, and love are strengthened. This is why God is pleased to be known and appreciated through miracles. And this is why we should not be brought low by life's sorrow and storms, for that is always the exact set of conditions when a miracle will take place.

XXXVII
The Desire for Wholeness Lives in All Souls

> This chapter presents again the paradox of Julian's vision: we will inevitably sin; we will turn away from God; we will become disjointed and distorted from God and our true selves—AND at the same time, we are kept eternally safe, whole, united with God.

God brought to my mind that I would inevitably sin. I was so taken up with the pleasure of looking at God, I could scarcely pay attention, but God waited patiently for me and gave me grace to focus my thoughts. This particular showing seemed to be directed particularly at me as an individual, but the comfort and grace that came from it, as you'll see, I was told to share with all my fellow followers of Christ—all in general, nothing in particular. When our Protector showed me that I would sin, however, that message was for me alone.

As a result, I experienced a vague sense of fear, but our Protector answered, "I am holding you safe." These words were spoken with more love, confidence, and spiritual safety than I can express. Even if I sin, the comfort that follows—safety and protection—belongs to all of us who follow Christ.

THE DESIRE FOR WHOLENESS LIVES IN ALL SOULS

What would make me love my fellow Christ-followers more than to see that God loves us all as though we were one soul? For in each soul God saves is a God-like piece, a volition that never said yes to separation from God and that never will. Just as there is a selfish, lower piece in us all that wills separation and disunity, so there is also a higher piece that wants only good. That is why we are that which God loves and that is why we continually do what pleases the Divine will.

Our Protector showed me this, the wholeness of the love where we live in the Divine sight. We are loved now, in this life, just as much as we will be when we stand in God's presence in Heaven. Our failure to love in this life, however, is what causes all our problems and pain.

XXXVIII
The Mark of Sin Is Turned into a Mark of Worth

The concept Julian asserts in this chapter may seem difficult: that sin could increase our worth. However, think of a human relationship such as a close friendship or a marriage: when we "make up" after an argument, don't we often find we are closer than we ever were before? And when our relationships survive years of disagreements and other wounds, they become far deeper, far more valuable to us, than they were at the beginning.

Julian speaks in this chapter of Saint John of Beverley, the seventh- and eighth-century Archbishop of York who founded the Anglo-Saxon monastery of Beverley, a double community of monks and nuns. During Julian's lifetime, John's feast day was celebrated on the seventh of May, which was the second day of her illness; this may be why he was particularly on her mind as she experienced her visions.

God also showed me that sin shall not decrease human beings' worth; instead, it increases it. For just as every time we separate ourselves from God we experience

THE MARK OF SIN IS TURNED INTO A MARK OF WORTH

pain, so too do we experience the joy of love's reconciliation after each separation. And just as each sin causes its own unique pain in this life, so shall its healing cause its own joy in Heaven in the same proportion that it caused sorrow on Earth. For each soul that reaches Heaven is precious to God, and the place is so filled with the worth and goodness of God, that no soul can come there without its sins being looked at and evaluated, and then that soul is endlessly affirmed and made known to itself and all Heaven, joyfully restored to its place of true worth.

During this showing, my awareness was lifted up into Heaven, and then God made me smile as the thought of David came to my mind, as well as many others, both in the Hebrew Bible and the New Testament: Mary Magdalene, Peter, Paul, Thomas and Jude (who carried the gospel to India), Saint John of Beverly, and so many others (too many to name). We know these saints' stories, we know that they sinned during their lives on Earth, and yet we do not think less of them, for we know that in the end, all was turned to their eternal benefit and worth. My thoughtful Protector showed all this to me: all I catch a glimpse of here in this life is revealed in its fullness in the life to come, where the symptoms of sin are changed to tokens of respect.

And as I thought of Saint John of Beverly, our Protector revealed him to me in greater detail, showing me the comfort I could find in this dear neighbor's life, which is so familiar and similar to my own. I heard God call him "Saint John of Beverly," just as we call him, and this made me glad, for I saw that Heaven grants him the same respect and honor we do. Then God reminded me that when John was still young, he had become God's well-loved servant, a person who loved and revered God greatly—and yet God allowed him to fall, keeping him safe all the while so that John was not destroyed, nor did he lose any time in his spiritual journey. And afterward, God raised him into favor that was multiplied many times. Because of John's bruised spirit in this life and his gentleness, God has drawn him into the many variations of Heaven's delight, where he knows greater joy than if he had never fallen. That this is true, God shows us on Earth with many miracles.

And all this was shown so that we would laugh out loud with love.

XXXIX
Our Bruises Bring Us to God

Julian continues to explain here how our wounds (our sins) are used in the Divine economy, where even the things that cause us shame become coins of redemption.

Perhaps this thought is so difficult for us because we think of sin as something tangible and concrete, a black and evil shape that comes between God and us, while the original biblical meaning was somewhat different. The word used in the Hebrew Bible meant simply "to err, to deviate from that which is straight or true." The Greek word used in the New Testament meant "to miss the mark," the same term used in archery when an arrow failed to hit its target. Our modern language often seems to define evil more sharply than goodness, as we saw with the word true ("that which is not false"). Meanwhile, earlier vocabularies defined sin and evil only as they related to goodness; from this perspective, you cannot understand or define what it means to "miss the mark" if you do not understand what that "mark" is. Apart from goodness, evil has no meaning.

*S*in is the sharpest scourge that can smite any soul; it is like a knife that scrapes off our skin, a whip that beats us to the point that we look hateful to ourselves, so that afterward we think we are good for nothing but to be buried in hell. And there we sink, until our bruises become the Holy Spirit's touch on our souls, and then sin's bite sends us leaping forward into God's mercy.

The Spirit's touch begins to heal our wounds, and our souls are revived as they turn to the Holy Church's life. The Spirit leads us to confess our sins, to reveal them in all their nakedness and truth, with such sorrow and shame that we have dirtied God's lovely image in our souls. Then we receive from our confessor penance for our sins, penance that is grounded in the teachings of the Spirit. This gentleness of spirit pleases God, and so does physical sickness that is sent by God, and also any external shame, sorrow, reproof, contempt, trouble, or temptation we might experience, either physically or spiritually.

With deep tenderness, our Protector keeps us, even when it seems to us that we are forsaken, as though we have been thrown out in the garbage because of our sin, just as we feel we deserve. The gentleness and humility that comes to us from this experience raises us in God's sight; our bruises give us compassion for others and a sincere longing for God. When we reach that point, we are suddenly delivered from sin and from pain, taken up into Heaven, and transformed into saints.

By our bruises and lacerations we are made clean, by compassion we are made ready, and by our sincere longing for God we are made worthy. As I understand it, this three-step process is how all souls come to Heaven, that is to say, all souls that have once been sinners on Earth. By these three medicines all our souls are healed.

And though our souls are healed, our wounds are still visible to God—not as injuries that diminish us but as marks of worth. As we are pained in this life with sorrow and regret, so shall we be rewarded in Heaven with the considerate love of our Protector God the Almighty, who honors us and wills that no part of the hard work of those who come to Heaven shall ever be wasted. For God views sin as a lover looks at his beloved's sorrow and pain; out of love, God puts no mark of blame on those who sin. The consequence of sin is not insignificant, but it is high, full of light, life, and worth for us all. And so shall shame be transformed into greater worth and deeper joy.

Our kind Protector does not want us to despair no matter how often or how badly we fall, for our failures do not get in the way of Divine love. Peace and love are always in us, living and working, but we do not always experience peace and love. Still, God wants us to pay attention and guard our minds with these facts: God is the ground of our entire life in love; God is our everlasting Keeper who defends us with total strength from our enemies, no matter how deadly and fierce they be—and the deeper our need, the greater our fall, the deeper and greater is God's grace.

XL
Safe Even in Sin

> Julian makes clear here that sin—missing the target God wants us to achieve—is serious business. Divine love keeps us safe even when we are separated from God, and yet, because of that love, any separation we experience becomes still more painful.
>
> Julian frequently refers to our Protector as "courteous and gentle." In Julian's day, both words were used to describe the king's court, considered to be a place of beauty and good behavior. I have replaced these with modern words that are closer to her original meaning: beautiful and kind.

This is the highest friendship of our beautiful, kind Protector, that we are kept safe so tenderly even while we are in the midst of sin. Christ touches us individually, in the private depths of our minds, and shows us our sin by the sweet light of mercy and grace. But when we see the pus and decay in our souls, we believe God is angry with us because of our sin. Then the Holy Spirit stirs our minds to life, our bruised souls turn to prayer, and we long with all our strength to put right our lives. We feel God is angry with us, and our feelings of guilt continue until our souls begin to find rest and our consciences grow easier. At that point, we hope God has forgiven our sins. And God has!

Our considerate and kind Protector reveals the Divine Presence to our souls; this Presence comes to us with laughter and a glad face, with a friendly welcome as if we had just come home after a painful prison sentence, saying, "My darling, I'm so glad you have finally come home to Me! In all your sadness, I was always with you, but now at last you see My love and we are united in joy."

This is the way sins are forgiven by mercy and grace. Our souls' worth is increased with joy, just as it shall be when we come to Heaven. This mercy and grace comes to us again and again, by the Holy Spirit's pleasant ways and by the strength and goodness of Christ's Endurance.

At this point, I truly understood that all sorts of things are prepared for us by God's great goodness, to such an extent that as we abide in peace and love, we are kept safe and whole. But because we do not fully perceive this in this life, we need to live in a constant state of prayer and yearning for our Protector Jesus. For He longs always to bring us to this fullness of joy (as I described earlier, in the showing of Christ's spiritual thirst).

Now, in the event that anyone is foolish enough to think that because we are offered all this spiritual comfort, we should go ahead and sin—or that we are less guilty—be careful! This is not the truth; these thoughts are the enemy of the true love that teaches us to hate sin. If my own feelings are any indication, I am certain that any soul in its natural state of connectedness to God will be more reluctant to sin the more it experiences Divine love—and when it does sin, it is far more ashamed because of this same love. For if all the pain of Hell and Purgatory and Earth—the agony of death, sickness, and every other trouble—were laid out before us side by side with sin, we would choose all that pain rather than sin. For sin is so ugly and despicable that it cannot be compared to any other pain. There is no deeper hell than sin. In fact, for the soul that is in its natural state of connection with God, there is no hell at all except for sin.

When we stretch toward love and gentleness, we are made beautiful and clean by the action of mercy and grace. God is as willing to keep us as safe as God is strong and wise. For Christ Himself is the basis of all human laws; He taught us to do good in the face of harm. He is Himself love, and He treats us the same way He teaches us to treat others. He wants us to be like Him, complete and whole in an endless stream of love toward ourselves and those who also follow Him. Just as His love for us is undisturbed by our sin, He wants our love for ourselves and others to continue undisturbed. But He wants us to endlessly hate all separation from God while we endlessly love the soul, just as God loves it. Then we will hate sin the way God hates it, just as we shall love the soul as God loves it.

Take constant comfort in what God told me: "I keep you safe."

The Fourteenth Revelation

XLI
All You Ask Is Grounded in Me

For Julian, the word "ground" meant that which is deepest and most elemental, the foundation of life and being. She insists that it is God who lives at the very-most bottom of who we are, and it is God who drives our deepest longings. In May Sarton's poem "When a Woman Feels Alone," she speaks of a similar concept, "the rootbed of fertility," connected to both our own hidden identity and also to the Divine.

This is a different slant on human nature from what mainstream Christianity has often taught. Many of us who grew up in the church learned that our human natures were deeply sinful; we distrusted our own longings, for we believed they would lead us astray; we labeled the yearning of our hearts as "temptation," something to be suppressed, resisted, disciplined. Julian is not saying we are unselfish and God-focused at our surface levels (at the level of our egos); instead, she is affirming that as we go deeper into our own being—digging down to the very foundations of our identities, listening to our truest and most elemental desires—we will find God's presence. When our prayer springs from this level, then it is God who prays through us.

After this, our Protector showed me insights into prayer. In this showing, I saw two perspectives on our Protector's meaning: one is the sense of rightfulness, that prayer makes us as we should be, stretched out straight and true toward God; the other has to do with our assurance that through prayer we are totally safe.

And yet oftentimes, our trust is incomplete, for we are not sure God hears us, or we think we are unworthy, or our emotions are empty (for many times we feel as barren and dry after we pray as we did before). Our foolish feelings make us weak. I know this from experience.

All these thoughts our Protector brought suddenly to my mind, showing me these words: "I am the Ground of each thing for which you ask. It is My will first that you have whatever it is, and then I make you yearn for it, and then you ask Me for it—so why would I not then give you that for which I have made you yearn?"

Our Protector gives us great comfort with these words. When the Divine Voice spoke this message, it revealed the endless reward we shall have for all our seeking. It is impossible that we should seek mercy and grace and not receive them. Each thing that we ask, God has already laid out for us from before the beginning of time.

This shows that we do not make God act with our prayers, as though we could move the Divine Essence to be what we want, but rather that the Divine lives in our true desires. This is what our Protector meant with the words, "I am the Ground." God wants all lovers of the Divine to understand this, for the more we grasp this truth, the more we will pray, pouring out our hearts' desires to God.

Seeking and asking is a true, joyful, and enduring soul-quality, a part of who we are as human beings, a quality that unites us and fastens us tight to the Divine Will at work in Creation by the sweet, internal workings of the Holy Spirit. First, Christ receives each prayer from us, and then I imagine He sets it in the Treasure House, where it will never fade away or perish. Our prayers rest there before God and all the Holy Ones, where they are continually received and endlessly answered, so that our needs become sources of prosperity that send us speeding forward toward God. When we reach Heaven, these prayers will be given back to us, delighting us as we thank God with endless worship.

Our Protector laughs with gladness at our prayers. He takes care of them and works through them to change our lives, for Divine grace makes us like God, not only because we are connected to Christ with the bonds of family love and relationship, but because we are becoming like Him. That is why God directs us, "Pray inside your minds, even if you feel no emotional satisfaction from doing so, for it is good for you, even if you can't feel the benefits, even if you can't see them, even if you think you are incapable of prayer. In the midst of dryness and barrenness, in your sickness and weakness, your prayers always make Me happy, even if you feel your prayer is flavorless and dry. I treasure all your prayers."

Because of the reward and the endless thanks God gives us, the Divine Will urges us to pray continually. God accepts our good intentions and our hard work, no matter how we feel emotionally. That is why we please God when we exert all our strength to pray and live united with the Divine; with God's help and grace, then, we keep all our abilities, our mental focus, our body's perceptions turned toward God, until we have what we seek, until our joy is complete, until we have Jesus. (Christ showed this to me in the fifteenth revelation, a little further on, when He said, "I am your reward.")

In addition, giving thanks is a part of prayer, a true heart-knowledge. When, with great reverence and loving awe, we use all our strength to turn ourselves to the work our good Protector inspires in us, our hearts fill up with pleasure and gratitude. Sometimes, this thankfulness becomes so great that it spills out of our minds into speech, and we cry, "Thank You, Protector! Blessed are You!" And sometimes when our hearts are dry and numb, or when the Enemy tempts us, we cry out loud so that we can hear in our own words the echo of Christ's Endurance and His great unity with God. Then the strength of our Protector's words spoken through our own mouths turns inward into our souls, bringing our hearts to life, leading them into Divine grace where they are restored to healthy function so that that our prayers become straight and true, exactly what they are meant to be.

Simply enjoying our Protector is the best thanks we can give.

XLII
Prayer Is a Taste of Heaven

> In this chapter, Julian continues to explain why prayer is such a necessary part of human life as God intended it to be. Prayer is "right," she affirms (straight like an arrow's flight), and prayer is "true understanding" (literally, in the oldest meaning of the word, something in whose presence we stand, something we are close to, and something with which we are united).

Our God wants us to live in the shelter of true knowledge, especially in three things having to do with prayer. The first of these is from whom and how our prayers spring to life. Christ told me from whom our prayers come when He said, "I am the Ground." And we see how they come to life in the centers of our being when He said, "It is My will first that you have whatever it is, and then I make you yearn for it." The second thing God wants us to understand about prayer is how we should carry it out. The answer to this is that we choose with all our mental powers to align our desires with the Divine Will; this is what He meant when He said, "Then I make you yearn for it."

The third thing we need to understand is the consequence of our prayers, their fruit: that we are united with God and made like Christ in all things. This was why this lovely lesson was shown to me. And Christ will help us, and we shall live out His words. Blessed may He be!

For God wants that both our prayers and our trust be large. For if we do not trust as much we pray, our prayers are emptied of worth, plus we make our own lives more difficult for ourselves. This is because, I believe, we don't really comprehend that our Protector is the Ground from which our prayers spring, nor that our desires are given to us by grace, by the generosity of Christ's love. If we grasped the reality of this, we would have total confidence that God will grant all that we truly desire. No one sincerely asks for grace and mercy without having already been given grace and mercy.

But sometimes it occurs to us that we have been praying a long time and have received no answer. We should not let ourselves be weighed down with these thoughts. I am certain that what our Protector wants us to understand from this showing is that either we must wait for a better time for what we desire or we must wait for a better gift. God knows the best match for all our desires. The Divine Will works to create a true knowledge of God in our minds, a comprehension of the Divine Essence in which all our thoughts and mental habits, all our intentions and the meaning of our lives have their foundations. On this Ground, God wants us to find our place, to build our homes there, so that we perceive all aspects of our lives by the generous light that falls from God.

The first thing we must remember is that God has made us shine; the second is that we have been redeemed in love, set free from all that would make us less than we are called to be; and the third is that God has given us Creation to enjoy, and out of love for us, the Divine Being keeps all things safe and secure. By showing me this, it was as if Christ were saying to me, "Look and see that I did all this before you even prayed. And now here you are, praying to Me!" He wants us to understand that the greatest acts of God have already been accomplished (just as the Church teaches), and as we meditate on this, we pray for the action that is already being accomplished: that God direct us while we live on Earth, so that God is enriched by our lives, and that we be brought to Divine joy in Heaven. And then God will have accomplished everything.

This is what Christ wants: that we see the Divine Hand at work even as we pray. For one without the other is not enough. If we pray and see no answer, we become weighed down with doubt, and that profits no one. But on the other hand, if we just sit back and see what God is doing and never bother to unite ourselves with the Divine Verb through prayer, then we are holding ourselves back, not investing in the work God is doing, and we diminish its action in our own minds.

But when our prayers and our awareness of God's work are united, we enrich the Divine Being and we ourselves prosper on our lives' journeys. Our Protector wants us to pray for everything, whether in general or in particular, that God has laid out to happen. As far as I can see, the thanks, joy, delight, and worth that God grants us in return is beyond our ability to comprehend!

For prayer is like an arrow shot straight toward joy's completion in Heaven—and prayer is also like a shelter that covers us with the knowledge that we can trust God to grant all for which we yearn. When we fall short of the joy that has been laid out for us, we are filled with longing; but as we cover ourselves with the knowledge of God's love and with sweet thoughts of our Rescuer, then we are granted the gift of confidence in God's firm integrity. As these two actions take place in our minds, we are continually in the Divine Eye, watched over by love. This is what we are owed in love, and God's goodness marks us with nothing less than the sign of love.

For our part, we must take care to always lovingly choose prayer as a way of life. We may still feel as though we have accomplished nothing—but in reality (whether we can see it or not), we have. And if we do what we can and ask with constancy and faithfulness for mercy and grace, then all that we lack we shall find in God. This is what Christ meant when He said, "I am the Ground of all you ask." With these words (words that God has highlighted) and with this showing, I saw that we can completely rise above all our weakness, doubt, and fear.

XLIII
Prayer Unites Our Souls with God

> Here we have a yet more in-depth description of prayer's importance. Julian explains that we are the ones who need to pray (rather than God needing us to pray). Prayer allows us to become active participants in God's creative action. As Julian says, prayer "matches our minds to God's."

Prayer makes the soul one with God. Our souls are like God in their essence, and they are connected to God with bonds of kinship—yet because of sin, our way of being is often not much like God's. That is why we need to use prayer as an affirmation that our souls are aligned with the Divine Will. What's more, prayer comforts our uneasy consciences and becomes a conduit for grace to flow into us.

That is why God teaches us to pray, and also to trust with all our energy and resources that our prayers will be granted. For God looks at us with love; God wants to make us partners in all the good the Divine Will accomplishes; and that is why we are inspired to pray for that which pleases God. And in return for this prayer and willing effort on our part (which are actually gifts from God), we are eternally rewarded.

This meaning was shown by the words: "And then you ask Me for it." God revealed so much pleasure and contentment in this sentence, as though God were in our debt for all the good deeds we do (and yet all along, it is the Divine Will at work through us), because we use all our mental faculties and physical strength to align ourselves with God's Will. It's as if God said, "What could possibly make Me happier than if you ask Me—with all your strength, with deep insight, and with total sincerity—to do the things I'm planning on doing?"

In this way, prayer matches our minds to God's.

But when our generous and considerate Protector through grace reveals the Divine to our souls, then we have all we desire, and our prayers are struck dumb. We cannot think of any other prayer, for we are so focused on the vision of God. In my opinion, this is a mountaintop form of prayer, a prayer that lies beyond our senses and human faculties. All the strands of our requests are pulled together into a single cord: looking at the One to whom we pray, the center and focal point of all prayer. Then we are filled with marvelous joy and reverent awe, such sweetness and delight that the straight lines of our various prayers become a single point: God. And there they remain, until the Divine Will once more stirs us to prayer for the details of our lives. And as I well know, the more we see God, the more we desire the Divine Presence in our lives by grace.

But there are many times when we cannot perceive God's presence in our lives, and then we go to Jesus, hungry and needy, reliant on prayer to enable us to go on. For when storms toss our souls, when we feel lonely and troubled, then we need to pray, so that we will become pliable in God's Hand, supple and responsive to the flow of the Divine Will. (Remember, though, prayer does not shape God nor do we channel the Divine Will so that it flows in one direction or another, for God is always the same in love.)

PRAYER UNITES OUR SOULS WITH GOD

This is what I saw: whenever we are aware of need, we pray—and our Protector (the Unity at the heart of all things that pulls us ever toward it) goes with us, strengthening our desires until, through extraordinary grace, we see God only. Then our awareness of all other needs drops away and now we go with God, while the Divine Will pulls us ever closer in love. For I both saw and felt that God's amazing and bountiful goodness makes complete all our abilities and strength. God's continual action in all sorts of things is so wise, so powerful, so unified and sweet that it is beyond our imagination, far past all we can believe or think. At that point, all we can do is look at God, filled with the joy of a mountaintop desire to be made one with the Divine—our entire lives centered in the Divine's dwelling place, where we too can be at home, taking pleasure in God's love and joy and goodness.

And then, by God's sweet grace, we shall continue in humble prayer, coming to God in this life with many private moments of spiritual insight and feeling, measured out to us in proportion to our ability to receive them. All this is brought about by the grace of the Holy Spirit, all through our lives and even as we die, filling us always with the longing to be loved. And then we will enter our Protector, and our selves will clearly know at last. We will fully have God, and God will have us, endlessly and totally. We will truly see God, fully feel God, clearly hear God. We will swallow God; we will drink God. (And how sweet is the taste of the Divine!)

And then we will see God face-to-face, completely, with familiarity and intimacy. The creature who was made will endlessly look at the Maker. In this mortal life, no human being can look at God and live—and yet, God gives us Divine glimpses that lift us higher than ourselves, strengthening us. God measures out these revelations as is best for us at the stage where we are.

More Thoughts on the Fourteen Revelations

XLIV
The Human Soul Reflects the Divine

> We are God's mirrors, says Julian, reflecting the Divine love, truth, and wisdom.

In all the revelations God gave me I saw that human beings are accomplishing the Divine Will, so that God's Being is made complete. And the Divine Will was demonstrated in the first showing, a marvelous example, where I saw its action in the soul of our joyful Lady, Saint Mary: the action of truth and wisdom. Now, by the Spirit's grace, I hope to explain how the Divine Will is accomplished.

Truth sees God, and wisdom grasps God, and out of these comes the third: an awed delight in God, which is love. Where truth and wisdom are truly present, then there is love as well, coming from them both. All this is a part of God's creation, for God is endless, supreme truth; endless, supreme wisdom; and endless, supreme love—self-existent, never made but always there, while the human soul is a creature that was made with the same properties as God. That is why the soul does what it was made for: it sees God, it grasps God, it loves God. And that is why God takes joy in a relationship with humanity, and humanity in endless awe with God. In this awe, the soul sees her God, her Protector, her Maker, so high, so great, so good, that in comparison, she feels as though she will drop into nothingness. But the clarity of truth and the light of wisdom make her see that she is made for love, a love where God endlessly affirms her.

XLV
Our Nature-Substance and Our Sense-Souls

Julian introduces two new terms in this chapter: our nature-substance and our sense-souls. In the 1300s, the word substance meant "essential nature," that which is inherent and innate, the qualities that make something most truly what it is (what the ancient Greeks called *ousia*, "being"). When Julian speaks of our nature-substance then, she is referring to our deepest essence, the thing that makes you you and me me. Our sense-souls, on the other hand, are closer to what Freud meant when he spoke of the ego, the self of which we are most aware, the identity that is linked to our physical experience of both the world around us and our own place there.

As Julian continues to struggle with her understanding of sin, these two concepts of the self help her integrate the Church's teachings with the eternal security she saw revealed in her visions. Sin, she reasons, affects our sense-souls—but not our nature-substance. Both aspects of human identity are real but at different levels.

God assesses humanity's worth based on our nature-substance, which is always kept unified in the Divine, endlessly whole and safe. The condition of our nature-substance is protected by God's unbending goodness, from which it was made.

But as human beings, we judge ourselves by looking at our changeable sense-souls, which seem like one thing this minute and another thing the next, depending on what we are paying attention to (whether the high things of life or the low), and these sense-souls are what we show the outside world. The perceptions of our sense-souls are a mixed bag, because we focus on so many different things. Sometimes life seems good and easy, other times hard and painful. The good and easy perspective is straight and accurate, but sin causes the hard and painful viewpoint. Our Protector Jesus, however, reshapes the troubles we experience in this life by the work of mercy and grace in our sense-souls, bringing all things straight and true.

These two perspectives are united at their hearts, and both shall be endlessly perceived in Heaven. The first viewpoint, based on God's perfectly straight ways as the Divine Presence stretches out without crookedness or bends, is because God's life is endlessly present in our substance. That is why in all the showings, I saw that God sees us as completely free of guilt and blame.

At the same time, though, despite the sweet and delicious taste of this realization, I could not be completely comfortable in my mind. This was because the Church's perspective on sin had been so real to me before these showings, and I did not know how to reconcile the two viewpoints. From the Church's teachings, I thought I understood that sinners sometimes deserve blame and punishment—and yet I could see neither of these in God. My sense of confusion and longing was more than I can tell. The higher perspective was straight from God, and I knew I must believe it—but at the same time, the Church had taught me the lower perspective, so how could I say it wasn't true? I yearned to understand how the Church's teachings are true in God's sight. Why would I have been shown something contrary to the Church? I wanted to reconcile the two perspectives in a way that would please God while it straightened out my confused thoughts.

I had no other answer but an image of a mistress and a servant, which I shall tell later [see chapter LI], and even that was vague and hazy. And so I continue with this longing in my mind, where it will be until I die, that by grace I might somehow make sense of these two contrary viewpoints.

For all of Heaven and all of Earth that belongs to Heaven are included in these two perspectives. And the more the Holy Spirit helps us to understand these two ways of looking at ourselves, the more we shall see and know our own failings—and the more we see them, the more, through grace, we will long to be fulfilled with endless joy and delight. That is how we were created to be, and even now, our nature-substance is always joyful in God. It has been that way since it was made, and it shall always be that way, world without end, no matter what our sense-souls may seem to say.

XLVI
A Paradox

> Again, many of us who grew up in the church learned that human nature was corrupted at the Fall that took place in the Garden of Eden—but Julian insists that our "nature" (which in the fourteenth century meant "essential qualities, innate disposition, inherent impulse or drive") is actually what drives us constantly toward God.
>
> Clearly, Julian is well aware that the established church of her day would find her ideas radical if not heretical. In this chapter she once more affirms her devotion to the Church, even as she also dares to say that there is no room in God for either anger or forgiveness, for nothing separates our "true selves" from the Divine Essence.

In the temporal life we experience here on Earth, our sense-souls seldom know what our true selves are. But when we truly and clearly see and know our own selves, then we will truly and clearly see and know our Protector God in the fullness of joy. That is why the nearer we are to our true bliss, the more we long for it, both because of our innate natures and because of God's grace. In this life we can only know the true self by continually using the power of our higher natures. And as we come to know the true self, we can exercise it and grow, as mercy and grace pushes us forward along the straight lines that lead to God—but we can never completely know the self until we reach that ultimate point where all lines meet, the point where this passing life and all pain and sadness reach their end. Our truest nature and God's grace make us yearn to know our selves in the perfection and completion of endless joy.

And yet in all this time, from the beginning to the end of the showings, I had two types of revelations. One was of never-ending love, utter security, and joyful safety, and these qualities were true of all the showings. The other, however, was of the Church's teachings, that which I had always considered to be the ground from which my relationship with God grew, which I had always disciplined myself to follow and understand as best I could. The showings did not take this away; they did not direct me to depart from the Church in any way; but instead, I learned to love the Church and be drawn to it even more than before, so that by the help of our Protector's grace I might grow and achieve a higher knowledge and love.

That is why in all the revelations I received, I believed I also needed to remember we are sinners who do much evil we should cease doing and who leave undone much that would be good. Because of this, we deserve pain and punishment—and yet I saw with such certainty that our Protector is never angry with us nor will ever be.

Our Protector is God: all that is good, all that is life, all that is truth, all that is love and peace. God's clarity and unity leaves no room for anger. I realized that Divine goodness and wisdom are such that they cannot contain anger. God is the goodness that cannot be twisted by anger for God contains nothing other than goodness. Our souls are made one with God who is unchangeable goodness, and so nothing exists between God and our souls, not anger, not forgiveness, for we are so completely united with God's Unity that nothing separates us from the Divine Essence.

Every showing I saw led me with love and pulled me with strength toward this same understanding of the Divine Nature. God wants us to understand this as much as we can. But there are other aspects of the Divine that God keeps hidden; we cannot grasp these realities until God helps us grow enough to do so. In the meantime, I am content to rest in our Protector's will for us—and yield myself to the Church as a little child would to her mother.

XLVII

We Become Misaligned When We Become Self-Centered

Julian elaborates further here on her understanding of original sin. She does not deny that it exists; instead, she makes clear that our mortal lives (our sense-selves) are deeply distorted from the shape God intended for them. And yet the pain and suffering we experience as a result of this are simply the consequences of this condition, rather than a punishment from God or an indication of Divine wrath.

Julian sincerely has no desire to overthrow the Church's teachings—and not only because she is afraid of being burnt alive! Her devotion to the Church is genuine. Instead, she is trying with all the focused power of her mind and words to unfold the Scripture's teachings, to examine the teachings of Christianity in their entirety, revealing their essence, their deepest, truest meanings.

Our souls have two duties: first, to marvel in awe, and second, to humbly endure, all the while enjoying ourselves in God's presence. For God wants us to understand that soon we will perceive all we desire within the Divine Reality.

But in the midst of this, I was amazed by what I saw, and I wondered, "What is the mercy and forgiveness of God?" I had always been taught that God's mercy was expressed when Divine anger at our sin was erased. I believed that for souls whose meaning and deepest desire is to love, the wrath of God is more difficult to bear than any other pain—and therefore, I understood that God's forgiveness must be the central point of Divine mercy. No matter how I searched to find this expressed in the showings, however, and no matter how much I wanted to find this, I couldn't find it anywhere in what had been revealed to me.

Instead, this is how I understood the work of mercy: Human beings are changeable while they live in this earthly life; because of their weakness and vulnerability they sometimes separate themselves from God. They are frail; they lack wisdom and insight; and their wills are easily swayed. On Earth, humanity lives in a storm of sorrow and pain, simply because we are blind—we cannot see God. If we could see God continually and clearly, then we would have no impulse to separate ourselves from the Divine Presence; none of our actions and desires would lead to sin.

I both saw this with my intelligence, and I experienced it emotionally at the same time. This understanding and emotion were higher, larger, and more full of grace compared to ordinary thoughts and feelings—and yet, I couldn't help but think how small and insignificant my sensations were next to the great desire we have to see God.

For I experienced five methods of action: enjoying, grieving, yearning, dreading, and hoping with absolute assurance. The enjoyment came because God gave me understanding and I knew it was the Divine Presence I experienced; I grieved because of my own failures; I yearned to see God more and more, know-

WE BECOME MISALIGNED WHEN WE BECOME SELF-CENTERED

ing we shall never be completely at rest until we see God clearly in Heaven; I dreaded the end of the showing, when my expanded ability to see would come to an end, and I would be left alone with myself again; and all the while, I had complete confidence in the hope of the endless love that will keep me safe by God's mercy and bring me to Divine bliss. The joy and the hope gave me such comfort that the pain of my grief and dread was diminished. And yet I understood through all this that my expanded vision could not continue into ordinary life, and I knew that this too increases our sense of God's worth even as it contributes to our endless joy.

We often lose sight of God. We become preoccupied with selfish concerns, and everything seems wrong. Our lives are no longer aligned with Divine joy; we feel as though our selves are at opposite poles from God, and this total disjointedness from the Divine Will is a part of our primal natures, rooted there by original sin. This is what causes our pain and storms; this is what makes us feel separated from God; and this is what yields earthly life's spiritual and physical pains.

XLVIII
Mercy and Grace Are Love's Two Faces

> Again, Julian explains here that sin has consequences; when we turn away from God, we are separated from peace and love. But the pain we feel is the result of our actions, not God's, and Divine mercy and grace step in to reverse even the natural consequences of our own failures.
>
> In this chapter, Julian introduces her thoughts on the expression of gender within the Divine, speaking of mercy as the outpouring of Divine Motherhood, while grace is the embodiment of God's Fatherhood.

But our good Protector the Holy Spirit, the endless life that dwells in our souls, keeps us completely safe. The Spirit works in us, creating peace and comfort, helping us to become once more aligned with the Divine Will, pliant and supple to the Spirit's wind.

This is mercy. This is how our Protector continually leads us, as long as we are here in this changeable life. I saw no wrath, except on humanity's part, and God forgives us for it. Wrath merely puts us off course from the straight roadway that leads toward

MERCY AND GRACE ARE LOVE'S TWO FACES

God; it makes us at odds with peace; it separates us from love. Anger springs up in our minds when we lack strength or wisdom, when we are fragmented and unfocused—but these failures are only in ourselves, not in God. Our sin turns us into outcasts from peace and love; it separates us from them. But God's face is always turned toward us. For love is the foundation of mercy, and mercy's action keep us safe in love. Grace and mercy were one, two sides of love's single face, in all I saw within the showings.

Mercy pays the price for our sin; it reverses what would have been the natural consequences of our separation from God. Mercy is sweet and generous, a work of love that mingles with abundant compassion. Mercy acts to keeps us safe, and mercy works to transform all that touches us into good. In love, mercy permits us to fail, and when we fail, we fall from God's presence; when we fall, we die, and this death is necessary whenever we lose sight and sense of the Divine Presence that is our life. Our failure is terrible, our fall is shameful, and our death is tragic—and yet through it all, the sweet Eye of love and compassion never ceases to gaze at us, and the work of mercy continues undiminished through it all.

I saw the substances of mercy and of grace, which are two methods of expressing a single love. Mercy is an act of compassion that expresses God's Motherhood, the Divine Feminine who is tender and loving, while grace is an act of Fatherhood, the masculine and kingly action that affirms our worth. Mercy shelters us, brings us to life, endures all pain, and heals us with infinite tenderness and love. Grace lifts us up, gazes at us with pride, and fulfills our desires with an abundance that is more than we deserve, spreading through our lives the plentiful generosity of God's royal protection and amazing courtesy. This is love's plenty, its largeness. Grace turns our terrible failures into full-bodied, endless comfort; grace transforms our shameful falls into leaps that carry us higher, increasing our worth; and grace works through our tragic deaths to bring us to life that is whole and full of joy.

I saw so clearly that as our contrary sinful natures bring us pain, shame, and sorrow here on Earth, grace produces still greater measures of comfort, worth, and joy in Heaven. When we finally reach out and grasp the sweetness grace has wrought for us, we will thank and bless our Protector, filled with endless gladness for all the woes we suffered on Earth. We will understand that we know God better in Heaven because of our trials on Earth.

And as I perceived all this, I had to conclude that God's mercy and forgiveness have nothing to do with Divine wrath; instead, mercy and grace diminish human wrath and gradually destroy it.

XLIX
Union with God Gives Peace

> In the New Testament book of James we are told that in God there "is no variation or shadow of turning" (1:17, YLT), and the Book of Hebrews affirms that Jesus Christ is the same "yesterday, today, and forever" (13:8). Julian's assertion that God does not "get angry" is based on this biblical understanding of the Divine Nature. Human beings experience a constantly changing emotional landscape, but God does not. The Divine Nature is eternal love.
>
> In Julian's vision, even the natural earthly consequences of our rebellion and sin are transformed, "sent to Heaven" where God changes them into eternal sweetness and joy.

I was amazed by what I saw in all the showings, but it was so carefully demonstrated again and again that I knew there was no mistake: our Protector God has no need to forgive us, for the Divine is not angry with us; it would be impossible for God to be filled with vengeful wrath. I saw that our lives are grounded and rooted in love; without love, we would not be alive.

When grace allows us to look into the amazing Divine Goodness, we see we are endlessly made one with God in love and it is impossible that anger separate us from Divine Love. For wrath and friendship are opposite forces. How could the One who erases and heals our angry arrogance, making us gentle and humble, be anything but unified in love, all gentleness and humility, which is the opposite of wrath?

I saw clearly that wherever our Protector appears, peace is present, and there is no room for anger and arrogance. I saw no anger in God at all, neither short bursts of anger nor long, enduring wrath, for truly, if God were angry even for instant, we would be destroyed, our lives and the very world where we live erased. As surely as our being is contained within God's endless strength, endless wisdom, and endless goodness, so we are kept truly safe by that same Divine strength, wisdom, and goodness. For although we feel our own frailty, and we experience dissonance and strife within our minds, yet we are in all ways enclosed by God's gentleness, humility, and kindness, by the Divine eagerness to give us joy. Our endless friendship with God, our life, our being, and our lives' homes are all contained in the Divine.

The same endless unity and sweetness that keeps us safe so that we do not perish, even when we turn away from God into sin, that same goodness continuously pulls us into a state of peace, despite our petty anger and contrary tendency to fall away from the Divine. This goodness makes us see our need, and we are filled with anxiety and turn to God, seeking forgiveness, longing for salvation. And though we are so often filled with anger and rebellion, which cause us to experience troubles, grief, and problems as we fall into our weakness and blindness, yet Divine mercy keeps us completely secure, and we do not perish. But we will only know that we are blissfully safe, possessing an endless joy, when we totally rest in peace and love, completely satisfied with God and the Divine Action at work in the world, at peace with our own selves and with all whom God loves, loving our own selves and all whom God loves, which is what Divine love wants for us. This is what the Divine's sweet unity accomplishes in us.

And so I saw that God is our true peace, our dependable Guardian when we fall from peace, and constantly at work to bring us to endless peace. Then, when by the work of mercy and grace we are made gentle and humble, we are completely safe— and suddenly, when we are at peace with ourselves, we find we have become one with God. For in God there is nothing that is not peace.

That is why when we are totally in peace and in love, we will no longer experience the rebellion and contrariness we do now. Our Protector, the Divine Goodness, makes all this to our profit. For our rebellion leads only to pain and sadness, but our Protector Jesus takes all that and sends it up to Heaven, where it is transformed into something more sweet and delectable than mind may think or tongue may tell. When we reach Heaven, we will find it there waiting for us, turned into true beauty and endless worth.

This is our God, the Ground that never shakes. The Divine joy will make us unchangeable, as God is, when we are there in Heaven.

L
Bringing Our Questions to God

> This chapter reveals again how genuinely pained and confused Julian is by the seeming contradictions between the Church's teachings and what she has seen in her vision. Nevertheless, the thoughts she expresses in this chapter indicate the security we have in God, the sense of comfort we should feel in bringing our questions and doubts openly into the Divine Presence.

In this life, mercy is the road we travel that leads us continually to grace. When we fall into storms and sorrows, we die, as is our destiny here on Earth, but meanwhile, in God's sight, the soul is kept safe, alive; it is not dead, nor shall it ever be.

All my soul's energy flowed into the wonder and awe I felt, and I thought, "Good Protector, I see You are the essence of truth, and I know that this is reality: we woefully fail You every day; we are guilty! I cannot escape the essence of who You are—and yet I cannot see that You blame us in any way. How can this be?"

For I knew from the Church's teaching and from my own sense of what is real that sin's guilt hangs over humanity continually, from the first human beings all the way through history until the day we are raised up into Heaven. I could not understand how our Protector God looks at us as though we were as clean and holy as the angels in Heaven. I tried to comprehend this paradox, these two realities that are such polar opposites, but no matter how much I pondered, I could find no resolution.

I worried I would lose sight of Christ's presence before I could understand this mystery. Either I needed to see that God had erased all sin, or else I needed to see how God regarded sin so I could look at it in the same way. My longing endured as I continued to look at Christ's figure in the showing, and yet I was impatient with my confusion and my inability to see clearly. On the one hand, if I concluded that we are not sinners after all, not guilty before God, then it seemed I would be mistaken, that I would miss the essence of what is real. But on the other hand, if we are guilty sinners...

Good Protector, why can't I see this in You, who are my God, my Maker, in whom I long to see the true nature of reality?

Three things gave me courage to ask this question: First, because the question is so humble. Second, because it is so ordinary, not secret or esoteric. And third, because I *needed* to know the answer (or so it seemed to me) if I were going to live my life understanding the difference between good and evil, loving goodness and hating evil, as the Church teaches. In my mind, I cried with all my strength to God, "Ah! Protector Jesus, King of All Delight, how can I find peace? Who will teach me? Who will explain the truth to me if I cannot seek it in You?"

LI
Double Vision

In Julian's original writing, the story she tells in this chapter is about a master and a servant, rather than a mistress and a servant. I took what is my greatest liberty in my translation of her book, and changed the gender. I did this for a couple of reasons: first, because it is consistent with Julian's overall message, that God is both masculine and feminine, and both genders can identify with the gospel story; and second, because changing the gender helps us achieve a fresher, sharper vision of what Julian is saying. Christ's message while he was on Earth turned upside down what the established religion of his day believed, and Julian's message was (and still is) equally radical and surprising. In the twenty-first century, we have greater freedom to express gender equality than Julian did, and I share her goal of startling readers with new images of God's amazing grace.

We also need to look at what the word "servant" meant to Julian. Like the word "lord," servanthood has come today to be associated with inequality and hierarchy; a servant is often considered to be someone who is inferior. Those who lived in the medieval era, however, did not think of "servant" as a demeaning term. Service was something employees rendered to their employers—but it was also what children offered to their parents, and lovers to their beloveds. It implied a sense of mutual obligation based on a reciprocal, consensual relationship. The one who served gained worth and identity from the relationship with the one to whom service was offered. In Julian's discussion of Christ as Mother, she further makes clear that the Divine Mother serves her human children; in other words, the service we offer God is returned to us as well.

In her discussion in this chapter, Julian reveals how her entire life has focused on analyzing and pondering the meaning of what she saw during her illness. Over the years, she explains here, she has come to see the servant as both Adam (All-Human) and as Christ. This joint identity helps her also make sense of the problem of sin, for we contain in our beings both Adam's fallen nature and Christ's eternal perfection.

And then our courteous Protector answered me with a hazy and wonderful vision of a mistress and a servant, where I understood the perspectives of both. In other words, I had double vision: both the mistress's view and the servant's view. I saw one of these spiritually but with a physical representation, while the other was only spiritual, without the physical aspect.

First, I saw two physical human beings, a mistress and a servant. The mistress was a stately person, sitting peacefully at rest, while the servant stood before her, ready to do whatever she asked. The mistress looked at her servant with love and kindness, and then gently asked him to run an errand for her. The servant leapt to do what his mistress asked; he set off running, eager to perform his mistress's request. So fast did he run, however, that he slipped and fell into a steep ravine. There he lay, groaning and moaning, wailing and flailing, struggling to get back on his feet. But he was helpless.

Through the entire vision, this sense of helplessness and loss of peace was the greatest fault that could be attributed to the servant. He refused to look to his loving mistress for help, though all the while, his mistress was nearby and could have easily helped him climb out of the ravine. But the servant brooded on his weakness; he wallowed in his misery.

Throughout this painful experience, the servant suffered seven injuries. The first was the deep bruise from his fall; the second was his sense of heaviness; the third, his weakness in the wake of the first two; the fourth, the loss of his sense of what was real, his mental blindness; fifth was his inability to get to his feet; the sixth—which was amazing to me—was that he was all alone, with no one else anywhere around him to help; and the seventh was that he had fallen in a hard and dangerous place.

I was surprised that the servant surrendered so easily to these hardships, and I watched him carefully to see if I could perceive that he was at fault in some way or if his mistress would blame him. Truly, however, I could not see how he was at fault in any way, for it was only his eagerness to serve that had caused his fall. Even now, he was as eager and committed as when he had stood before his mistress, ready to do whatever she asked. As a result, his loving mistress still looked at him with the same tenderness.

And now I began to see with the double vision I mentioned earlier: first, I watched the servant, feeling pity and compassion for him; and at the same time, I understood what the mistress was feeling. With the eyes of my spirit, I saw that the mistress was filled with gladness, because she already had a plan to save her servant. The queenly mistress said to herself, "Look at the trouble and pain my beloved servant has suffered because of his love for me and his intention to serve me. Wouldn't it be appropriate if I rewarded him for his fear, his suffering and injury, and all his grief? Even more, shouldn't I give him a gift that will make his life even surpass what it would have been if he had never fallen into this trouble? Would not this be grace?"

During this internal spiritual showing, the meaning of the mistress's words sank into my soul, and I saw that the nature of the mistress requires that the beloved servant not only be rewarded for his trouble but lifted even higher than he would have been had he never fallen. His failure and sadness will be transformed into ultimate worth and endless joy.

At this moment, the vision disappeared, and our good Protector led me on to the end of the showing. I continued to marvel over this example, however, for I believe God had given it as an answer to my longing to understand the apparent dichotomy between the Church's teachings and what I had seen in the showings. At the time, however, I did not have a chance to ponder what this example fully meant.

If the servant is Adam, then I saw too many and varied qualities in him for him to be considered a single person. At the time, I continued on in confusion, for I could not yet fully understand what I had seen. Looking back, I see that this single vision revealed three perspectives. Even though I continue to understand more and more about the showings, each of them also continues to be filled with mysteries that have not yet been unfolded.

It seems right to me to explain the three perspectives I have come to understand, which have somewhat eased my confusion.

The first is the beginning of the lesson I understood while I was watching the servant and his mistress; the second is the understanding I have gained as I have pondered it since then; and the third is the entire revelation from beginning to end, everything that is contained in this book, which our Protector God brings often and freely to my mind. At this point, the three perspectives are so united in my mind that I can no longer separate them one from another. Together, they have taught to me to believe and trust in our Protector God, that the same Divine goodness demonstrated during these showings will also reveal to us their meaning.

For nearly twenty years after these showings, I continued to be spiritually instructed. The message I always heard was this: "You must study all the conditions and aspects of the example you saw, even though they seemed to be hazy or insignificant." I eagerly committed myself to this goal, and mentally studied the vision, going as far as my intelligence and understanding would take me.

I began by looking at the mistress and the servant, and I considered how the mistress was sitting and where she sat; the color of her clothes and what they looked like; her expressions and the sense of internal goodness she exuded; how the servant stood and where; what the servant's clothes looked like; and the servant's outward demeanor and inner desire to serve his mistress.

I understood that the mistress who sat in such stately rest and peace was God. I saw that the servant was Adam—or from God's perspective, All-Human. For God sees all humanity as one human, and one human as all humanity; even though we are individuals, we cannot separate ourselves from each other. This All-Human's selfhood had suffered a terrible blow, as though a battering ram had slammed against him. That which had made him most strong was struck down, so that he became weak; his intellectual insights were deadened and diminished, so that he could no longer see the presence of his mistress. And yet all the while, his mistress saw his intentions as whole, and for this his mistress praised him. In himself, he had no sense of his own intentions; he was separated both from his mistress and, in a sense, from himself, so that he could not perceive the same reality the mistress saw. When we truly see both God and ourselves, then we shall find rest and peace. In this life, any experience we have of this is a partial one at best, but in Heaven, this experience shall become complete by God's grace.

I understood now how God looks at our sin. It is only our own pain that makes us feel guilt. This is our only punishment, for our courteous Protector comforts us and sorrows for us. The Divine Presence brings only gladness and love.

In the vision, the mistress simply sat on the ground, in a wild, deserted place. Her clothing, however, was rich and luxurious, as would be appropriate for a wealthy mistress; it was a beautiful, sad, blue color, the aching blue that makes tears come to your eyes. Her expression was one of mercy; her skin was brown with features that were full and pleasant; her eyes were black and filled with compassion, and I could tell she could see both far and wide, as though her gaze encompassed the endless heavens. But all the while, the love with which she watched her servant never ended, and I thought such love might melt our hearts and break them into two, so mingled was it with compassion and joy. The compassion was directed toward Earth, caused by the great fall of the beloved All-Human, while the joy was directed Heavenward, focused on Christ's presence beside the Creator. The Divine mercy looked down on Earth and made it complete; it went with the All-Human into Hell, and it kept him safe there, protected from endless death. This mercy and compassion lives with humanity until we rise to Heaven.

But human beings are blind in this life, and we cannot see the Creator God's reality. The only glimpses we can catch of the Divine Presence are the ordinary ones, where God is revealed in ways to which we can relate, as though God were another person like ourselves. Despite this, I do not think we should reduce the Creator God to the level of a human being; we should not anthropomorphize the Divine One in this way.

The fact that the mistress in my vision sat on the ground in a wild and lonely place meant this: God made humanity's soul to be the Divine City, the Home of God, the place most pleasing to God of all Creation. But when humanity falls into sorrow and pain, so that the human soul can no longer serve its proper function, our Protector and Creator will take no other place to be the Divine Home. Instead, the mistress—God—sat on the ground, so she could be as close as possible to humanity whose form is mingled with the Earth, until the time when Jesus restores the Divine City to its rightly beauty through His labor and suffering.

The blueness of the mistress's clothing symbolized her unchanging commitment to the servant; the brownness of her skin showed her earnest dedication; the length and breadth of her clothes, which billowed around her like a flame, indicated that she had enclosed within her all Heaven, all joy, all gladness. And all this was shown in a mere moment, and then my understanding was led inward, as I described earlier, so that I saw the mistress's joy at the abundant restoration her grace will bring to her servant.

And yet I still marveled as I looked at the mistress and the servant as I have just described them, the mistress so stately and the servant standing in humility before her. In the servant, too, I experienced a double understanding: Externally, he was dressed simply, as an ordinary laborer ready for work, as he stood close to the mistress but off to one side (rather than straight in front of her). He wore a white coat that was old and worn, stained with sweat, threadbare and a little too small for him. It looked like something ready for the ragbag, which surprised me: why would such a well-loved servant wear clothes like this in the presence of so worthy a mistress?

Internally, however, the servant was filled with a love that mirrored the mistress's. The servant knew there was but one thing he could do that would enrich the mistress's worth, and without thought for himself, the servant set off to do this thing. His outward clothing indicated he had been a servant who had worked hard for many years, but his internal thoughts seemed to indicate he was new to the job, filled with the eagerness of someone who is fresh and ready.

I saw that the Earth held a treasure the mistress loved. I wondered what this could be, and then it came to me: it was some kind of food, something delicious and sweet. The mistress sat there with no food or drink, and no one to serve her except the one servant who had hurried on his way. As I watched, I tried to think what the servant's job must be, and I realized he must do what is the hardest job: he was a gardener, someone who must dig and delve, toil and sweat, turning the earth upside down to seek the deepest soil for his plants' roots, then watering the plants when they needed it, making sweet floods stream over them. This work endured until the plants yielded their fruit, which he could then bring to the mistress, serving her all she desired. But the servant could not turn back until he had prepared this food exactly as it would best please the mistress—and then he would bring her the food and drink. All this time, the mistress would sit there waiting for the servant.

I marveled at these thoughts, for I saw that the mistress had everything contained within her—endless life and all manner of goodness—and yet she lacked that one treasure only the servant could bring her. The treasure was grounded in the mistress, rooted in her endless love, and yet she needed the servant to bring it to her. Without the mistress, there was nothing but an empty wilderness, but it was the servant who brought fruit and food to the mistress. I could not comprehend what this could mean.

And then I understood: The servant is All-Human, but he is also the Second Person in the Trinity, the Child, Jesus. The Child is part of the Divine Essence with the Creator, but He is also All-Human. The mistress is the Creator God; the servant is the Child, Jesus Christ; and the Spirit is the love that flows between them and from them both. When Adam fell, so did the Divine Child, because the two were united in Heaven, and God's Child could not be separated from Adam. (By Adam, I mean All-Humanity.) Adam fell from life to death, into the deep valley of this world, and from there into Hell; meanwhile, the Child God fell with Adam into the Maiden's deep womb, she who was the fairest Daughter of Adam, so that Adam would be pulled back to Heaven, released from Hell.

Through all this our good Protector revealed that the Divine Child and Adam are one Being. The strength and goodness we possess is the Christ in us, while the blindness and weakness is Adam. Both of these aspects were revealed in the servant. Our good Protector, Jesus, has taken on Himself all our guilt, and therefore the Creator God can no more blame us for our sin than could Jesus Himself be blamed. The Child, Jesus, the servant, stood before the Creator, waiting to be sent into the world to do that which would bring All-Humanity to Heaven. This does not mean that Jesus is not at the same time God, just as the Creator is God, both aspects of the One. But the Child also knew He would be a human being, to save humanity in fulfillment of the Creator's plan, and so the Servant stood before the mistress, eager, ready to do His job. As soon as He was sent out, He hurried on His way, and then He fell (into the Maiden's womb), but He thought nothing of His pain or suffering.

His white coat stands for Christ's flesh, the only thing between the Divine Essence and humanity—an old, tight, stained garment that shows how long All-Humanity has labored in poverty and effort. It was as though Jesus were saying, "Look, my beloved Parent, see I stand before You dressed in Adam's clothes, ready to get started, ready to run to do Your will wherever You send me. How much longer must I wait?"

Of course the Child knew the answers to these questions, in as much as the Child is part of the Divine Essence, the Wisdom of the Creator, but these questions demonstrated the understanding of All-Humanity, whose perception is limited by time and space. But all human beings—we who are saved by the incarnation and effort of Christ—are the Humanity of Christ. Christ is the Head of this Body of which we are all members, but the members do not know when sorrow and suffering will come to an end, and everlasting joy and delight shall be completed. This is the moment for which all the Company of Heaven longs, and those of us who are under Heaven come there by means of our longing and desire. (Longing is the road we travel, and desire is our road map.)

This longing and desire was expressed in the way the servant stood before the mistress (which at the same time expressed the Child's standing before the Creator clothed in Adam's garment), for humanity's longings and desires were made visible in Jesus. Jesus is All-Humanity who shall be saved forever, and All-Humanity (the part of us that will be saved) is Jesus: the Love of God, all that humanity possesses of humility, strength, goodness, patience, and obedience.

This wonderful example was given to me the way a teacher shows a child the ABCs, for the letters will eventually help the child understand so much more. For the entire revelation's secrets are contained within this small and hazy example (although of course all the showings are filled with mysteries).

The way the mistress sat speaks of the rest and peace that belongs to the Divine Essence, for while God cares for Heaven and Earth, there is no effort, no labor, no suffering in the Divine work. The fact that the mistress stands for God shows that God has authority over humanity. The way the servant stood off to one side indicates that he sprang from the Divine Essence but in his action and effort he was All-Humanity, for Jesus came from this Essence, then fell into Mary's womb and became a member of the human family. This fall was not an easy one; human flesh pained Him, for it carried death. His fall injured him; His wound was our flesh, which caused Him to feel death's pain.

The fact that the servant stood off to one side indicated that his clothing was not appropriate for him to stand face-to-face with his mistress. This would not be his role so long as he was a laborer, nor could he sit down and rest in his mistress's presence until he had earned his peace through his hard work. He stood to the mistress's left side because God willingly allowed the Child to suffer humanity's pain. The servant's ragged and torn clothing symbolized the tearing and shredding of Christ's skin with blows and scourges, thorns and nails. The way the servant struggled and writhed, moaned and groaned, unable to get to his feet again, speaks of the way in which Christ yielded His soul into God's hands from the moment He fell into the Maiden's womb until the moment He died, identifying Himself completely with All-Humanity.

Once He died, however, He began to show His strength once again, for He went into Hell, where He raised up the great company of souls from the deepest depths, which merged with Him in highest Heaven. His body lay in the grave until Easter morning, and after that His weakness ended forever.

Our Rescuer transformed humanity's weak and mortal flesh, Adam's worn-out clothes that had become outgrown and tight, into new clothes that were clean and bright, comfortably long and luxuriously loose, far more beautiful and rich even than the clothing the mistress wore. Her clothes were blue, but the servant's clothes were a mingling of colors more marvelous than anything I can describe, for it was a treasure too great for words.

Now the servant no longer sits in the dirt in the wilderness; instead, he relaxes in a comfortable seat he made for himself in Heaven. He no longer stands to one side, humbly, dressed in worn-out clothes; instead, he and the mistress are face-to-face, and he is dressed in clothes that are blissfully comfortable, while he wears a jeweled crown on his head.

And I understood that we are Christ's crown, and this crown is God's joy, the Child's worth, the Spirit's satisfaction, and the endless and amazing gladness of all those who are in Heaven. The servant's reward is long and wide, full of the deepest Heavens, and the Spouse, God's Son, is at peace with His beloved Wife, who is endless joy. In the Eternal City, the Child's Divine Essence is united in rest and peace with All-Humanity. The Creator has set everything in order, dressed Creation in the clothes it was always intended to wear: the Creator in the Child, the Holy Spirit in the Creator and the Child.

LII

We Have Reason to Mourn —and Reason for Joy

> Here Julian elaborates still further on the meaning of the double perspective she discussed in the previous chapter. Our role, Julian says, is to be aware of sin in our lives, to examine ourselves carefully for anything that clouds our vision of God—but that is not the Divine role, for God looks totally past our sins and sees us as whole.

And in all this I saw that God rejoices that He is our Father, and at the same time She rejoices that She is our Mother. God rejoices that He is our True Spouse and our souls are His beloved Wife. And Christ rejoices that He is our Brother, and that He is our Rescuer. These are five of the utmost joys, and I understood that God wants us to share these joys: praising, thanking, loving, and endlessly blessing God.

All of us whom Christ has rescued have within us a marvelous mingling of health and wounds, wholeness and sorrow, for we contain in our beings both Jesus our Risen Protector and Adam, who fell into death. In Christ, we are kept steadfastly safe; the

WE HAVE REASON TO MOURN—AND REASON FOR JOY

touch of His grace on our lives raises us into the certainty of our safety—but at the same time, we are terribly broken, our emotions and vision shattered by Adam's fall, so that we experience pain, sin, and darkness.

But in our deepest essence we continue to abide in God, faithful and trusting in the Divine mercy and grace; this is the Divine work functioning within us. Divine goodness opens our eyes to true reality, but our vision fades in and out, sometimes sharp and sometimes blurry, as God allows. We are raised into the One, even as we are permitted to fall into the other.

This mingling of life and death, rising and falling is so strange that we cannot even know where we truly are, for our perceptions are so sundered from each other that we can't tell what is real. On the one hand, we live in a holy agreement with God; when we feel the Divine Presence in our lives, we set our wills, our intellects, our souls, and our strength to following God. Then we hate the arrogant stirrings in our minds, all that causes us to fall away from God, physically and spiritually. But then again, we lose sight of the Divine sweetness, and we fall once more into such darkness that we stumble into all manner of sorrows and troubles. We can only comfort ourselves that we never give our deepest permission for the trouble and sorrow to enter our lives; the strength of Christ our Protector guards our inmost beings. We revolt against the darkness, our minds filled with groaning, enduring the pain and sadness, praying for the time when the Divine Presence will once again be revealed to us.

This is the medley of human life: faith and sorrow, insight and darkness, joy and agony, singing in counterpart through our days. But God wants us to know that through it all the Divine Presence is the melody that never changes. Christ is with us in Heaven as the True-Human who draws us with Him ever upward (as was revealed in the showing about spiritual thirst); God is with us on Earth, leading us (as I saw in the third showing where I saw God as a single Point); and God is within our souls, endlessly dwelling there, keeping us safe, directing us, drawing straight lines for us to follow all the way to Heaven (as was shown to me in the sixteenth showing, as I will describe later).

In the vision of the servant, I saw the injury and blindness of Adam's fall, but the servant also symbolized the wisdom and goodness of Christ, God's Child. The mistress in the vision demonstrated the mercy God feels for Adam's grief, but she also revealed the honor and worth All-Humanity will reach by the strength of Christ's Endurance and death. The Divine delights in both humanity's leaps and falls, knowing that our falls lead us to a greater joy than we could have ever known otherwise. And so even as I watched the servant fall, I was led into the highest awareness of God's honor and worth.

That is why in this life we have reason to be sad, for our sin caused Christ's pain—but we also have eternal reason for joy, for it was Christ's endless love that made Him suffer. And therefore we created ones, we who are given the grace to see and feel the work of love, hate nothing but sin, anything that comes between God and ourselves. In my opinion, love and hate are true opposites, immeasurably separated from each other.

Despite the love that remains in our deepest essence, I saw that in this life we stumble into sin. In Heaven, we shall be cleaner and purer than we are here—and yet throughout this life, grace keeps us safe from sins that would lead us to eternal pain (the mortal sins of which the Church teaches), even as we do our best to avoid venial sins (those that are easily pardoned), as much as we are able.

When we stumble in our blindness and weakness, the sweet touch of grace nudges us back to our feet, and we shouldn't

WE HAVE REASON TO MOURN—AND REASON FOR JOY

hesitate to get up as fast as we can. Then we fix our attention on the Church's teachings and proceed on our way, confident of God's love despite the pain of our sin. This attitude means that when we sin, we neither wallow in despair nor do we become reckless, treating sin as though it didn't matter; instead, we honestly acknowledge our weakness as we stand naked before God, accepting that in our own strength we cannot keep our balance for even the blink of an eye. All we can do is humbly cling to God, trusting the Divine Presence to be our only strength and safety.

God's viewpoint is totally different from humanity's. As human beings, it is our role to search out our sins and weaknesses, examining ourselves with deep humility—but meanwhile, the role of our Protector God is to look past all our weakness, calling us upward into Divine goodness and unity. It is these two perspectives that were revealed in the vision of the mistress and the servant: the outward reality was one of weakness and humbleness, while the inner reality was that of endless love. Our Protector wants us to search our selves earnestly and diligently, so that we become fully aware of our failures and their consequences, understanding that we can never be whole without God's everlasting love and abundant mercy.

This double awareness—of both our weakness and our total security in Divine love—is what our Protector asks of us, and it is this that the Divine Presence brings to life in our hearts. Both realities are true: the lower, external reality and the deeper, inner reality. Human beings have fallen into terrible darkness and pain—and all the while, they are eternally protected, their beings fulfilled in the Divine.

But the higher reality touches the lower one as well, for all life and strength we experience in this life (the lower reality) comes down to us by grace from the deepest essence of our High Selves. No real distance lies between the lower life and the higher, because it all springs from a single love. This love has a double function in our lives: in the lower life, mercy and forgiveness give meaning to our pain and endurance, while in the higher life, there is nothing but a single, pure love, a marvelous joy that heals all our earthly wounds.

Through all this, our Protector showed us that not only are we excused from all blame in God's eyes while we live in this life, but once we are united with the High Self, all our failures will be turned into an endless treasure.

LIII
Endless Love

> At that hidden, intimate point where our souls spring to life, there we are knotted tight to the very being of God. The word "knot" that Julian uses here could, in the fourteenth century, also refer both to marriage and to a paradox, a difficult problem that has no apparent resolution. This sense of paradoxical union—wholeness in the midst of brokenness, a unity between God and humans that is as real as the separation—is at the heart of Julian's message.

I realized God wants us to understand that from the Divine perspective, any human failure is no worse than Adam's original sin—and we know that Adam was endlessly loved, kept safe during his time of need, and now he is joyfully restored to the utmost joy. Our Protector is so good, so considerate, and so kind, that we are seen as faultless, and through us God is ever blessed and praised.

Through this understanding, which I gained from the showing, my confusion was eased. I realized in every soul kept safe by God there lives a will that never agreed to be separated from the Divine, nor ever will agree, despite the appearance of external circumstances. This aspect of the human soul is the Divine Will living in us, a sense of volition that is so good it can never say yes to the presence of evil; instead, it always leans toward goodness, and it works for the unity of all things in the sight of God. Our Protector wants us to be assured of this reality, that a piece of our very essence remains whole and safe in Jesus Christ, our Divine Protector. In Heaven, all created beings will be knit tight to God, fulfilled by the Divine alignment and unity—but this will only be possible because all along a part of our deepest substance was never separated from God, nor ever could be because of the Divine Vision, endless and unlimited, that works with the Divine Will, drawing straight lines toward the single Point where all is One.

But despite this alignment and unity, the straight lines that lead always into wholeness, humanity's redemption and restoration are still necessary in everything, essential for our prosperity and well-being, as our faith teaches us through the Church. For I realized that God never began to love humanity; just as human beings are intended for endless bliss, fulfilling God's joy that flows through creation, so in exactly the same way, humanity was always known by God and always loved, without any beginning. The intent of Christ, the Holy Go-Between, was always aimed directly toward this goal of endless love. The Trinity was in agreement with this intention, their Divine "Yes" spoken from before the beginning of time. The Go-Between is the Founder of the human family, the Source of our nature and life, from whom we all spring, the Womb that encloses us all. We shall all wind our way into this Go-Between, finding there our total Heaven, our everlasting joy, just as the Trinity intended all along.

God loved us before we were made, and when we were made, we loved God. This love is made out of the Holy Spirit's substance and nature, made purposeful by the strength of God the Parent, and made wise by the vision of God the Child. At the same point where our souls spring to life, created by God from God, there we are sewn tight to God.

The human soul was made from nothing; that is to say it was brought into being from nothing that had previously been created. When God made the human body, however, the Divine Hand used the Earth's clay, solid matter that is a mixture of all the tiny pieces that make our world. So we are both Nature-made—and at the same time, we are not-made. And what is the only thing that is not-made? God! That is why God truly lives in each human soul, with nothing between the Divine Essence and ours.

In God's endless love, our souls are kept whole; this is what all the showings demonstrated, this is what they each meant. In this endless love we are led, kept safe in God, and we will never be lost, for our safety is inherent in the moment and method of our creation. God wants us to be aware that our souls are alive, filled with life that shall endure without end, thanks to God's goodness and grace. In Heaven, we shall endlessly love God, thank God, praise God. And just as our lives will have no end, in God we were treasured and hid, known and loved, without any beginning.

God's highest creation is humanity, and humans find in Christ our fullest essence and ultimate strength. Our souls are knit tightly to God at the deepest level of their being, with a knot so delicate and strong that our souls become one with God, made endlessly whole and clean and safe. God wants us to know that all souls kept safe everywhere are eternally rescued by this same knot, made one in this unity, made whole and healthy through Divine health.

LIV

Faith Is Merely This: Believing We Are in God and God Is in Us

The radical assertion Julian makes here—that God lives in our souls as we live in God—does not set up human beings as God's equals, for she insists that even as we are united with the Divine Essence, "only God is God," while humans are God's creation.

At the same time, the unity she describes is not one where the human soul loses its individuality. The word "enclosed," which she uses over and over throughout this chapter, implies that we retain our individual beings, even as we are united with God. (We are not "absorbed" by the Divine, nor do we "dissolve" into the Divine, but rather the word implies that we are embraced, nourished, held, and loved.)

In this chapter, Julian returns once more to the concept of the sense-soul and nature-substance. Many philosophers and modern psychologists have used a similar concept, but Julian's is somewhat different. Most psychological models equate our consciousness with our identity, so that our psyche and our physical beings are separated, but for Julian, our consciousness is linked to our physical beings, and both are separated from the substance of our true identities. As a result, our awareness is cut off from knowledge of our own substance; we cannot perceive our truest natures, except through the eyes of faith.

FAITH IS MERELY THIS: BELIEVING WE ARE IN GOD AND GOD IS IN US

And because of the great and endless love that God has for all humanity, God makes no distinction in love between the Soul of Christ and the smallest rescued soul. It is easy enough to believe that Christ's Soul dwells in the Divine Essence—but it follows then that where Christ's Soul makes its home, so do all the souls He rescues.

We should take great joy in the fact that God lives in our souls—and even more joy in the fact that our souls live in God! Our souls were created to be God's home; and our souls' home is God, who was never created. God who is our Maker lives in our souls, and our souls live in the Divine Essence, the very substance from which we were created. Thus, I can see no difference between the Divine Essence and our own: all is God. Yet let's be clear: only God is God, and our essence is a Divine creation that lives within God.

This is the all-powerful truth of the Trinity: that our Father made us and keeps us safe in Him; this is the wisdom of the Trinity: that our Mother encloses us in Her wisdom; and this is the goodness and unity of the Trinity: that we are protected. We are enclosed in the Divine, and the Divine is enclosed in us. The Holy Parent-God lives in us, and so does the Holy Child-God and the Holy Spirit: All-Strength, All-Wisdom, All-Goodness: one God, one Protector.

Our faith is a strength that the Holy Spirit brings out of our nature-substance into our sense-soul, and through this faith, all other strengths come to us. Without faith, we are weak, for faith is merely a straight and direct understanding (a true belief, a deeply rooted trust) in who we are: that we are in God, and God—whom we cannot see—is in us. The strength that faith yields in us accomplishes great things, allowing us to live as Christ's children.

LV
Christ Erases Humanity's Double Death

If we follow the spiritual path Julian points us toward, we will not reject the human condition but embrace it. At the mysterious point where our souls and our flesh are connected is the Divine Home, the City of God, the place where God lives and never leaves.

Greco-Roman philosophies left their fingerprints on Christianity (and on the entire Western world), marking our minds indelibly with the concept of dualism—we are body and soul, good and evil, male and female—but Julian suggests that an innate unity is deeper than any dichotomy we experience between ourselves and God, between our bodies and our spirits (and between male and female). God is present in the sensual world just as much as God is in what we sometimes think of as the "spiritual" world, and both together form the soil that nourishes the substance of our being. In Julian's vision, all separation becomes false as it disappears in the Point that is eternity's single Now.

In this chapter and in others, I chose to use the word "Child" in place of "Son" when referring to Jesus, in order to create more gender-inclusive images.

CHRIST ERASES HUMANITY'S DOUBLE DEATH

Through all this, then, Christ is our Way. He leads us safely in His laws, and His Body carries us up to Heaven. For I saw that each of us of who are saved by Christ lives within Him (we are His Body), and thus He gives us to God the Parent in Heaven, a present that the Parent receives with deep gratitude. And then the Parent-God turns around and generously gives back the gift of our souls to the Child-God, Jesus Christ. This reciprocal gift gives joy to the Parent, bliss to the Child, and pleasure to the Spirit. (This was seen in the ninth showing, where I spoke more of the homes where God resides.)

Of everything that we do in life, this is the most pleasing to our Protector: that we share in the Trinity's circle of joy through the strength and work of our salvation. Despite our up-and-down feelings of sadness and happiness, God wants us to understand and hold tight to the belief that our being exists more in Heaven than it does on Earth.

Our faith springs up from the love we have for our body's physical senses, from reason's clear light, and from the very structure of our minds, a gift God made us at our creation. At the same moment that our souls were breathed into our bodies, we at once became clothed with both our senses and with mercy and grace. Divine compassion and love cared for us, as the Holy Spirit shaped through our faith the hope that we shall rise to our truest essence, into the strength and goodness of Christ, enlarged and fulfilled through the Spirit.

I understood through this that our sense-souls are rooted both in this world and in Divine mercy and grace; this is the soil that nourishes us, enabling us to receive the gifts that lead us to endless life. I saw clearly that the essence of who we are, the very substance of our identities, is in God, and God is in our sense-souls.

For at the exact point where our souls are connected to our flesh and senses, at that same point God built the Divine City, the Divine Home, a resting spot God never leaves. God never departs from our souls; the Divine Essence lives there with eternal joy. The sixteenth showing demonstrated this: Jesus will never leave the place He takes in our souls.

God has given creation many gifts, and all these are also given to the Child Jesus. Jesus keeps these gifts safe; they are enclosed in Him as He lives in us until we have grown up enough to enjoy them. Our souls grow with our bodies, and our bodies with our souls, each lending support to the other, until we are mature, as our natures dictate. And then, as we continue to grow, rooted in the soil of this world, nourished with Divine mercy, the Holy Spirit breathes into us the gifts that lead us to endless life.

Through all this, God led me to the understanding, the vision, and the knowledge that our souls are created trinities, reflecting the image of the joyful Trinity that was never created but has always existed. We are known and loved without any beginning, and we were created within the unity of the Maker. This vision filled me with sweetness and wonder, as well as peace, rest, and a delicious sense of safety.

Because of the treasure of unity that God made between our souls and our bodies, humankind shall be restored out of double death into life. This restoration could not be complete until the Second Person of the Trinity took on the physical substance of humanity's nature, which is based on the perceptions of our five senses while at the same time our highest essence had been made one with God from the moment of creation. These two aspects of humanity are in Christ, both the higher and the lower: a single

Soul. The higher-self lives always in peace with God, in complete joy and delight, while the lower-self, the sense-based nature, suffers on the Cross for humanity's redemption.

I saw these two aspects of Christ in the eighth showing, when my body was filled with the sensations and emotions of Christ's Endurance and death. Remember how a friendly voice suggested that I look up into Heaven, but I could not? This was because the vision of the inner life was so strong: the private reality that lives within each soul, the life that is the high-substance, the Soul of Christ, which rejoices endlessly within the Divine Essence.

LVI
Our Sensual Nature and Our Spiritual Essence Are United

For Julian, true self-knowledge and God-knowledge are two strands of a single cord. Contemplative theology has traditionally affirmed that the quest for self-knowledge leads to God, but Julian looks at this from another slant that implies the value God puts on human growth: God-knowledge, she indicates, allows us to integrate our sense-souls with the knowledge of our true essence, our nature-substance.

She goes still further and suggests God approves when we enjoy our own souls the way a lover would commune with a beloved. This is not navel-gazing that Julian is recommending, but an egoless relationship with our own identities that is based on the humility of genuine love. This concept is difficult for us, so steeped are we in both the egocentric perspectives of our world and at the same time the fear of selfish arrogance that religion so often teaches us.

Julian presents yet another radical concept: the soul, she says, is not merely our "spiritual side" but it is equally our physical, sense-based identity. Our eter-

OUR SENSUAL NATURE AND OUR SPIRITUAL ESSENCE ARE UNITED

> nal essence is made up of both. According to Julian, the separation we have been taught to see between these two "sides" of our being is a false one that never existed.
>
> And yet at the end of this chapter, she comes back full circle: the sense of separation we feel between our physical and spiritual selves forms the space that mercy and grace fill–and so, even in our state of alienation and blindness, God is blessed (and so are we).

Through all this I saw that it is easier for us to come to know God than it is for us to know our own souls. For our souls are rooted so deeply in God, where they are so endlessly treasured, that we cannot truly know them until we first know God, the Soul-Maker, with Whom our souls are united. Nevertheless, we have a natural tendency to wisely and earnestly seek to know our own souls. As we do, we also find God, and by the Spirit's grace and guidance, we come to know both God and our own selves. And so it doesn't really matter, whether we are moved to seek God or our souls, for both these desires are healthy and true.

The Divine Being is nearer to us than our own souls, for God is the soil in which our souls are rooted; God is the Midpoint that unites our eternal substance and our sense-souls, so they can never be separated. For our souls sit at rest in God; our souls stand up straight in God's strength; and our souls' very natures are rooted in God's endless love.

That is why, if we want to understand our own selves, if we spend time communing with our souls and enjoying them as a lover enjoys her beloved, it makes sense that we also seek the Divine Protector, in Whom our souls are enclosed. (I understood more about this from examining the sixteenth showing, as I shall explain later.)

What is a soul? These visions showed me that our spiritual essence can be rightly called our soul—but at the same time, our sensual natures are also our soul. This is because of the unity they have in God; we may see them as two separate things, but they are not. Our Protector Jesus sits in the homestead of our sense-soul, where He is enclosed, and all the while our natural essence is enclosed in Jesus, while the Soul of Christ sits at rest within the Divine Essence.

It is only right that we should feel longing and a sense of lack, a need to change and become something more so that we will be led so deep into God that we can truly know our own souls. Our Protector God leads us deeper and deeper, higher and higher, with the same love with which we were made, the same love Jesus showed in His mercy and grace through His Endurance on the Cross.

And yet despite all this, we can never clearly know our own souls until we fully know God. Until our souls have come into their complete strength and abilities, both physically and spiritually, we will not be totally whole—and that will not happen until our sense-souls, by the strength of Christ's Endurance, are immersed in the Divine Essence through the fruits of our own earthly trials, which our Protector makes ripe through Divine mercy and grace.

OUR SENSUAL NATURE AND OUR SPIRITUAL ESSENCE ARE UNITED

I had caught a glimpse of what it means to experience the Divine touch on my soul, but this touch is not something out of the ordinary; it is grounded in the very nature of our being. Our intelligence is rooted in God, the substance of our truest nature, and from our nature, mercy and grace spring and spread through us, accomplishing in our lives the fulfillment of our joy. This is the soil in which we grow and become complete.

These are the three properties contained in a single unity, and where one is at work in our earthly lives, all are at work. God wants us to understand this, so that our minds are consumed by the longing to understand more and more, until the time when we are complete. To fully understand all this is nothing but the endless joy and delight of Heaven—and this joy and delight begins here on Earth because God wants us to begin to know Divine love here, in this life.

Our intelligence alone cannot carry us far enough; we need equal amounts of both meditation and love. Our natural substance, though it is rooted in God, would not be enough either, were it not for the mercy and grace that grows from that same soil. From these three working together—our natural substance, mercy, and grace—we receive all our goodness, our unity. Our primary gifts are properties of human nature, for when we were first made, God gave all these properties to our natural substance. And then the Divine Being gave us still greater purpose, for God's endless wisdom wanted us to be double beings, with twofold natures. The space created by our sense of separation from ourselves is the space where mercy and grace grow.

LVII
Our Two Natures Are One in Christ

Spiritual asceticism calls for the separation of our "spiritual" natures from our sensual experience, but here Julian insists that Christ unites our physical and spiritual experience into a single identity. Only in Christ, she claims, does human selfhood become a coherent whole.

According to Julian, Christ was joined with humanity even before Creation. To think otherwise, she indicates, would be to imply that the Divine who is eternal experienced temporal change. And yet Christ the eternal also chose to enter time; Jesus of Nazareth was born in a particular year in a particular place. It is another paradox: Christ is both unchanging and eternal AND he has a specific place in time (like light as seen by quantum physics, he is both a wave of endless motion and a particle, a specific point). As humans, we too partake of paradox: we are both Christ and Adam, both Divine and fallen from grace, both eternally safe and constantly (in this life) experiencing the effects of sin.

Julian's thought here is similar to that of some of her contemporaries. Walter Hilton, another medieval mystic, wrote in his *Ladder of Perfection*:

OUR TWO NATURES ARE ONE IN CHRIST

The better you find Jesus, the more you shall desire Him. . . . You have lost Him, you feel, but where? Truly, you have lost Him in your own house, that is to say, in your soul, . . . for He is still in your soul, and never is He quite lost from it. . . . He is in you, though He be lost to you, but you are not in Him, till you have found Him. This is also His mercy, that He allows Himself to be lost only where He may be found, so that you have no need to run to Rome or Jerusalem to seek Him, but only turn your thoughts into your own soul where He is hid. . . . But perhaps when you seek Jesus within your soul, you find only darkness. . . . Do not waste your time studying this dark image, which is your sinful self, I tell you, for it is no thing. . . . Truly it is nought, or no real thing. . . . This nothing is nought else but darkness of conscience, and a lack of the love of God and of light; as sin is nought but a want of good. . . . And here also you must beware that you take Jesus Christ into your thoughts against this darkness in your mind, by busy prayer and the fervent desire for God, not focusing your thoughts on that Nought I have described, but on Jesus Christ whom you desire. . . . For within this Nought is Jesus hid in His joy . . . but this darkness of conscience, and this Nought is the image of the first Adam.

God gave nobility and richness to our very substance, so that we shall always do the Divine Will, proving God's worth. (When I say "we," I mean all those who are safe in God.) For I saw that we are truly that which God loves, and we do that which pleases God, forever, without any limits, because of the great riches, excellence, and abilities given to our souls and knotted to our bodies. These knots are what make us sense-creatures (beings who perceive reality through our senses).

This is why in our truest essence we are complete, even while our sense-souls fail. All these failures God will restore and make complete through the work of mercy and grace, which flow from the essence of the Divine Nature. The Divine Essence makes mercy and grace active in us, and our own essence, which God gave us, enables us to receive their actions.

I saw that our nature is whole and complete within God. From this wholeness flow out the unique variations that work God's will, and all the while our very natures keep us on track, while mercy and grace restore us and complete us. No part of our nature shall die, for the highest aspects are tied to God from the time they were made, and meanwhile God is fastened to the lower aspects of our natures from the moment of our conceptions (the moment when our souls took flesh), and thus through Christ, the two aspects of our natures are united.

For the Trinity is contained within Christ, and in Him our higher-part is grounded and rooted, while Christ, the Second Person of the Trinity, took on our lower-part and made it His own, as it had been assigned to Him eternally by His very nature. I saw very clearly that all the Divine works that have ever been accomplished or ever shall be were always and endlessly completely foreknown by God. Out of love, God made human beings, and that same love became a human being.

The first property we receive from God is faith, and from this source flows all our progress. Faith springs from the lofty riches of our nature-substance into our sense-soul, and it is rooted in us through the very essence of the Divine, by the working of mercy and grace. From this come all the other human properties that lead us and keep us safe. Even the commandments of God are included within our faith, which we should understand in two different ways: first, so that we can understand, know, and seek what God wants for us; and second, so we can avoid that which God does not want. Our human lives are included under the covering of these two ways of thinking. Also, the seven Sacraments are contained within our faith, as God appointed them, as well as all manner of strengths and abilities.

The same abilities we received through our human essence, imbued into our natures by God's Unity, these same abilities are also given to us and renewed by the Holy Spirit in grace through the action of mercy, and then these abilities are also kept safe and treasured by Jesus Christ. For at the same time that God was fastened to our human bodies within the Virgin's womb, the Divine Essence put on our sense-soul. By this action, human beings became enclosed in God, and the Divine Essence became united with our own. In this unity, God is the perfect human being, for Christ knotted to Himself each individual and thus became the Complete Human, the essence of all humanity. Because of this, Mary is also our mother, and in her we too are enclosed and borne (and then born); she who is the mother of our Rescuer is also mother of all who our Rescuer saves—but at the same time, our Rescuer is also our truest Mother, the One who bears us endlessly.

All this was shown to me with such fullness and sweetness, but it had been referred to even from the first showing, where I saw that we are all enclosed in God and God is enclosed in us. This Divine enclosure is also spoken of in the sixteenth showing, where I saw that God takes a seat in our souls.

It is God's delight to make the Divine Kingdom within our intelligence; to repose at rest within our souls; and to dwell there endlessly, so that we all function within God, our actions making us God's helpers as we pay attention to God, learn the Divine information, keep the Divine laws, desire that all actions be God's actions, and truly place our trust in God.

For I saw that our truest essence is in God.

LVIII
Nature, Mercy, Grace

> Julian develops here a practical and experiential understanding of our connection to the Trinity.

God, the blessed Trinity (endless Being whose purposes stretch out as unswerving lines without end or beginning), always contained the thought of humanity. The human family was structured for God's own Child, the Second Person of the Trinity. And when God was ready, the Divine created us, with the full support of the entire Trinity, and in our creation we were tied to God, our being knotted to the Divine. This union keeps us always as clear and noble as we were when we were first made, and the strength and goodness of this union allows us to love and seek our Maker with praise, gratitude, and endless delight. This is the work that is accomplished continually in every soul Christ rescues, the will of God.

That is why Almighty God is the Father of our nature; God, All-Wisdom, is our Mother; and with the love and unity of the Holy Spirit, the Trinity is all one God, one Protector. In our union with God, God is our True Spouse, and we are the Beloved.

This marriage will never be divorced, for God says, "I love you, and you love Me, and Our love shall never be broken."

I saw these three properties at work in the Trinity: the Fatherhood, the Motherhood, and the Protection, all One God. The Almighty Father keeps our natural substance, our sense-self, safe and joyful, as it was always, without beginning or end. Meanwhile, the Second Person's intelligence and wisdom keeps our eternal souls alongside our sense-souls, restoring us and rescuing us, for Christ our Rescuer is both our Mother and our Brother. Our good Protector, the Holy Spirit, watches over us and makes our lives and labor worthwhile, surpassing all we could desire, for the Spirit's graciousness and courtesy is amazing, exalted, and bountiful.

Our entire life is threefold: in the first aspect, we have our being; in the second, we have our growth; and in the third, we have our fulfillment. The first is our nature, the second mercy, and the third grace. The Trinity's high strength is our Father; the Trinity's deep wisdom is our Mother; and the Trinity's great love is our Protector. These Three are ours, woven into the nature and substance of our being.

What's more, I saw that the Second Person of the Trinity is the Mother of both our eternal essence and our sense-soul. God made us with a dual nature—both a spiritual and a sense-based being. The spiritual essence is the higher part of our nature, given to us by the Father, God Almighty, nurtured in us by our Mother, the Second Person of the Trinity, in whom we are grounded and rooted. The Second Person is a merciful Mother who shares our sense-based nature and keeps our duality united and whole. In Mother Christ we are nurtured so that we grow, and in Mother Christ's mercy we are reshaped, restored, reunited with our spiritual essence, through the power of Christ's Endurance, Death, and Resurrection. This is our Mother's work in all of us who yield ourselves to Christ.

Grace works with this maternal mercy, a work that springs from the Third Person, the Holy Spirit, who vigilantly guards us and generously gives to us. We receive a generous portion of truth, a reward that is given freely from grace, beyond anything that is merited.

In this way, we have our being in the Father, God Almighty; while we are remade and restored in our Mother of Mercy, made whole and perfect; and all the while we are fulfilled in the Spirit's grace, as we yield ourselves to our Protector. The substance of our being is in our Father, God All-Strong, and it is in our Mother, God All-Wisdom, and it is in our Protector, the Holy Spirit, God All-Goodness. For the essence of our being is complete in each Person of the Trinity, who is one God, but our sense-souls dwell only in the Second Person, Jesus Christ (but God the Creator and the Holy Spirit are one with Christ). In Christ, by Christ, we are pulled from Hell, we are lifted up from Earth into Heaven, where our sense-souls are joyfully united with our spiritual essence. There we grow greater with the wealth, nobility, strength, and goodness of Christ, by the grace and action of the Holy Spirit.

LIX
Christ Is the True Mother

> The Greek philosopher Plato described what he referred to as Forms, the objective blueprints of reality that lie beyond the phenomena our senses perceive: the ideal, unchanging shapes of all that we know in this life. Using a similar line of thought, Julian asserts in this chapter that Christ is the "True Mother," the ideal embodiment of Motherhood, the perfect Mother-pattern that gives meaning to all human motherhood. Although other medieval theologians spoke of Jesus as a mother, Julian carries this concept further than any other. She insists that Divine Motherhood is as inherent to God's nature as is Fatherhood.

Mercy and grace grant us all this joy. If all goodness (all that is whole and desirable) were not contained in God, we would never experience this joy. Human knowledge was allowed to go against that which is good, but the unity of mercy and grace worked against this misalignment and then transformed it into something valuable and good for all those whom Christ rescues.

The Divine Nature does good in the face of evil, and it is in this way that Jesus Christ is our truest Mother, for from Christ springs our life (as it did with our human mothers), and Christ's sheltering love follows us continually throughout our entire life. Yes, God is our Father—and yes, God is also our Mother. The Divine demonstrates this in all that exists, saying, "I am the strength and goodness of Fatherhood; I am the wisdom of Motherhood; I am the light and grace that comes from all true love; I am the Trinity; I am Unity; I am the authority of goodness living in all things. I am the One who makes you love; I am the One who makes you yearn for more; and I am the endless fulfillment of all true desires."

Where the soul is at its lowest, humblest, and gentlest, there it is also at its highest, noblest, and worthiest. From this reality grows all our sense-soul's strengths; they spring up from this soil naturally, and mercy and grace water them, or we would never grow. Our High Father, God All-Strong who is Being, knew and loved us before time existed. This Divine knowledge, alongside a deep and amazing love, chose with the foreknowledge of the Trinity the Second Person to become our Mother. This was our Father's intention; our Mother brought it about; and our Protector the Holy Spirit made it firm and real. For this reason we love our God in whom we have our being. We thank and praise our Father for our creation; we pray with our entire intellects to our Mother for mercy and understanding; and we ask our Protector the Holy Spirit for help and grace.

In these three—nature, mercy, grace—are contained our entire life. From these we have gentleness and humility; patience and kindness; and we turn away from sin and human arrogance. Our truest strength relies on this turning away. And in this way Jesus is our True Mother, the Mother of our human nature, that which we were created to be—and Jesus is also our True Mother by grace, because He chose to take on our human nature. All the qualities of motherhood come from the Second Person of the Trinity, where we are kept whole and safe, both in our human nature and by spiritual grace, fed by Christ's particular goodness.

I understood that we can consider God's Motherhood from three perspectives: the first is that the Divine Mother gave birth to us and gave us life; the second is that She shared our lives; and the third is that She works always to keep us safe. Through the Divine Mother, grace is spread out wide and long, deep and high, like a blanket that has no edges or binding.

And all is one love.

LX
The Loving Mother

> If Julian did not experience motherhood firsthand, then her relationship with her own mother must have been close and rewarding. However, her words in this chapter make it seem very likely that she was in fact a mother herself, for she expresses with a deep and intimate understanding the physical experience of birth and nurturing, an experience she relates completely to her understanding of Christ. But Julian takes this one step further: motherhood IS God, she asserts, and physical childbirth is as much a Divine process as is spiritual birth.

This is a good place to say more about what I understood our Protector to mean in regards to the limitless blanket of grace. The Motherhood of mercy and grace restores us to our true natures, that which we were made to be by the Motherhood of love, the Motherhood of being. This motherly love never leaves us.

Our Mother by nature, our Mother by grace, wanted to become our Mother in all things, and so Christ planted the seeds of Divine action in the humble and gentle soil of the Maiden's womb. (Christ showed me this in the first showing, where I saw how humble this girl Mary was when she conceived the Divine.) In other words, the High God, Sovereign Wisdom, put on flesh and mothered us in all things.

A mother's help is the most intimate, the most quick to respond, and the most certain: most intimate, because it is tied to our simplest biological natures; the most quick to respond, for a mother's love is an automatic and instinctive aspect of her being; and most certain, because it lacks all artifice or pretension. Our human mothers bore us into a world of pain and death—but our True Mother, Jesus—All-Love—bears us into joy and endless life. (Blessed may She be!) In this way, Mother Christ supports and holds us in love within Herself (as a pregnant mother holds her unborn child).

No one else could mother us the way Christ does. Christ's labor pains were suffered on the Cross, where we were birthed into joy. And Mother Christ was willing to suffer still more for us, but Jesus could not die again, and so like all mothers, our Mother fed us, not with milk but with the Body of Christ, the Blessed Sacrament, the food of life. This is what Christ meant when He said, "I am the One whom the Church preaches and teaches. In other words, all the health and life found in the Sacraments, all the strength and grace of Scripture, all the goodness found in the Church, all that is Me."

A human mother holds her child tenderly to her heart; our loving Mother Jesus leads us *into* the Divine Heart, where we see the Essence of God, the joys of Heaven, and the certainty of endless delight. This is what I understood from the tenth showing, where Christ said, "Look! How I loved you!"

The word "mother" is so sweet and intimate that it cannot truly be used to describe anyone except Christ. Motherhood is the essence of natural love, wisdom, knowledge—and motherhood is

God. God is as much in the physical process of labor and delivery as God is in the process of our spiritual birth.

Any natural, loving mother knows and understands her child's needs; she watches out for the child with vigilant tenderness. As the child grows, the mother's care changes but not her love. At some ages, the mother may allow the child to experience pain so that the child will grow in maturity and grace. In the same way, our Protector works in us. Christ is the Mother of both our human nature, our sense-selves, and our spiritual being, and sometimes our sense-selves must suffer so that our spiritual beings grow. Our Mother wants our love to be focused on Her.

And in this I saw that anything we owe to God's Fatherhood and Motherhood is fulfilled when we truly love God—and Christ makes this love grow in us. This was revealed in all the showings, but especially when Christ said, "It is Me Whom you love."

LXI
Divine Love Can Never Be Broken

> In this chapter Julian describes still more clearly our Divine Mother, Christ. As we read her words, we catch a new glimpse of what it means to be loved by God, a vision that is grounded in our human experiences of mothering and being mothered.

While God was giving birth to our spirits, the Divine kept us safe and whole with a tenderness like no other. Our souls are priceless treasures in God's eyes, and so God kindles our understanding, directs our ways, eases our consciences, comforts our souls, lightens our minds, and makes us love all that God loves and be pleased with all that pleases God (as we come to know and hold dear the joyful Essence of the Divine, as well as Christ's sweet humanity and blessed Endurance, marveling at God's high and overflowing unity and sweetness).

And when we fall, God quickly lifts us up, leaping out into our lives like a mother playing peek-a-boo with her child, reassuring the baby with her touch. And when we have been strengthened by God's action in our lives, then we choose with all our consciousness to serve God and be God's lovers, endlessly.

But sometimes God allows us to fall further and harder than ever before (or at least it seems that way to us). When that happens, we (who are still so foolish) feel as though we've accomplished nothing, that all our spiritual journeys have been delusions. But this is not reality. We need to fall sometimes—and we need sometimes to feel our failure. If we did not, we would not know how weak and exiled from our true selves we are, nor would we truly understand how much our Creator loves us. When we reach Heaven, we will clearly see how terribly we separated ourselves from God—and how despite that, Divine love for us never diminished nor did we ever become less precious in God's eyes.

Our failures are trials that yield a high and marvelous awareness of God's endless love. Love that cannot be broken when it is wounded is both amazing and strong. This knowledge is one benefit of our failures, and the other is the humility we gain, a lowness of spirit that lifts us to Heaven on a road we might never have found otherwise. That is what we need to understand in the midst of our failures—and if we miss out on this understanding, then our failures will do us no good. Most of us, though, fall first and only later come to understand that we are still held safe in God's love; our failures and our understanding are both contained within the mercy of God.

A mother may allow her child to experience pain sometimes, when it is for the child's good—but she will never willingly allow the child to be in any real danger. Our earthly mothers may not be able to protect us from death (no matter how much they long to), but our Mother Jesus will never allow Her children to die, for She is All-Strong, All-Wise, and All-Love, as no one else can be (blessed may She be!).

But often when we realize our failure and exile, we are so terribly afraid and ashamed of ourselves that we can scarcely stand ourselves. But our kind Mother does not want us to run away from Her when we feel like this; that is the last thing She wants! Instead, She wants us to be like a hurt and frightened child who runs as fast as he can to his mother. That is how Christ wants us to respond to our own failures, saying, "Mommy, Mommy, I've made myself dirty and I'm not like You anymore, and I don't know what to do. Help me!"

If our fears are not immediately eased, it is only because our wise Mother knows we need to mourn and weep for our failures a little longer, and so, with tenderness and pity, She allows us to do so. God wants us to be like a child who trusts his mother's love, whether he is happy or sad, healthy or sick.

God also wants us to find our Mother in the Church's faith, so that we can be comforted by the understanding of our fellow God-Lovers. A single person may often feel as though she is broken into pieces, but the entire Body of the Church can never be broken. That is why it is a good thing to be humbly and deeply fastened to and united with our Mother the Church, who is the Body of Christ Jesus. For the food of mercy—Christ's blood and water—is bountiful, making us beautiful and clean; our Rescuer's wounds are ever ready to offer us healing; and our Mother's loving hands are always diligently caring for us.

Christ is like a loving Caregiver who has nothing to do but pay attention to the well-being of Her charge. It is Her work to keep us safe; it is Her honor to work for us; and it is Her will that we know what She is doing, for She wants us to love Her and trust Her with both humility and strength.

Christ demonstrated this with His words: "I will take absolute care of you."

LXII
Always Safe

> Julian makes clear her own humanity. We can relate to her experience of self-hatred—"all the ways we negate our true selves, the ways we scorn ourselves and throw ourselves away"—and with her, we can find comfort in Christ's "glad friendliness," his tender care and transforming love.
>
> The word "naughty," which we have come to think of as a word for childhood misbehavior, came from the root words Julian uses here. Would our children understand the concept of "naughtiness" in a different way if they thought of it as anything that makes them less than their true selves?

During this showing, Christ showed me our weakness and failures, all the ways we are broken, all the ways we negate our true selves, the ways we scorn ourselves and throw ourselves away, all the sighs and sadness we might ever experience in this life. And in the midst of all this, He demonstrated His glad friendliness, His strength, wisdom, and love. In all our times of trouble, He takes care of us as tenderly as He does during those times when we feel most happy and soothed, honoring Himself by keeping us always safe. In our brokenness, He lifts us spiritually into Heaven, and transforms all our failures into His honor and our endless joy. His love keeps us safe, so that nothing is ever lost.

All this comes from the Divine Essence, the Unity of God, by the working of grace. The Divine Essence fits all things together perfectly and sweetly; it is the substance of reality, the essence of all that is. God is reality. God is the true Father and the true Mother of all that is; the substance of all things flows out from God to work the Divine Will, and when humanity is rescued by grace, all shall be restored to what it was meant to be in God.

Some portion of the Divine Essence lives in many forms in many creatures, and it is expressed fully in human beings, in strength, beauty, and goodness, in nobleness and dignity, in majesty, worth, and honor. We are all God's debtors because our most primal substance springs from God, and we are also God's debtors because Divine grace has rescued us. We do not need to search afar to find God's Essence expressed in the world around us; instead, we find it close at hand, in the Church, at Christ our Mother's breast—and in our own souls, where our Protector lives. There we will find all faith and understanding, and in Heaven's delight, we will at last see God clearly.

But we should not take pride in our Divine qualities, as though they were unique to us alone. Instead, they come to us all from Christ; the Divine Essence was designed in Him so that human beings could share His dignity and worth. This was the joy of humanity's rescue, which Christ always knew, without any beginning.

LXIII
Sin Is Unnatural

In this chapter, Julian again affirms that Nature (including human nature) is inherently good. In Julian's original writing, she uses "kinde" instead of "nature," an Old English word that meant "innate nature, character, quality derived from birth." Meanwhile, during Julian's time, the word "nature" had only recently arrived in England from the Latin language, via the French Normans. Etymologists tell us that at the beginning of the fourteenth century, the word meant "essential qualities, innate disposition," and also, "the creative power in the material world." By 1386, during Julian's lifetime, the word had expanded to include "inherent, dominating power or impulse." All these meanings add nuance to Julian's words here.

Christianity has historically often claimed that Nature (with all the meanings the word encompasses) was corrupted at the Fall, but Julian insists otherwise: grace is God, she says, and Nature is also God. They cannot be separated. Based on these realizations, she reaches this conclusion: sin—separating ourselves from God—is deeply and terribly unnatural. It goes against the very grain of who we are, it negates the reality of our identity.

SIN IS UNNATURAL

> This chapter also contains further explanation of Julian's view of Christ as our "True Mother," as well as her affirmation of a childlike perspective. "Only when we reach the Father's glad and friendly Presence," writes Julian, "will we climb again as high as we do in childhood." As Jesus said in the Gospel of Matthew, "unless you change and become like little children, you will never enter the kingdom of heaven" (18:3, NIV).
>
> The word Julian frequently uses to describe God's Fatherhood is "bliss," a word whose meaning has shifted over the centuries. The Old English word (which was grounded in the Germanic languages) carried in it connotations of "kindness, gentleness, happiness, brightness, friendliness, sympathy, and joy." Julian's image of God here (and throughout her book) is so positive and appealing that it seems light years removed from the frightening, distant, patriarchal image some of us grew up imagining. Julian affirms the masculinity of the Father Creator (even as she speaks of the femininity of Mother Christ), but this is a "glad and friendly" father, rather than a disapproving or intimidating one.

We hate sin, both naturally and by grace. For Nature—all that has been born into life—is good and beautiful. Nature went out from God, and then grace was sent out to bring Nature back home and destroy all that would undo it, to bring Nature back to the holy Point—God—from which it first came, even more noble and worthy now, because of grace, than it was in the beginning. All who are in God's Presence, all those who have been made whole in endless joy, will see that Nature has been tested in pain's fire, and that it has not flaw or fault. In this way we see that Nature and grace are in agreement, for grace is God, and Nature is God. God works in two ways, but Divine love is united and singular. Nature and grace cannot be separated; they work together.

When, by God's mercy and help, we too are united with Nature and grace, we will see that sin is truly more ugly and painful than Hell, for sin—going against God—is contrary to our nature. Sin is not only dingy and unclean; it is unnatural. That is why it is such a horrible sight for the beloved soul who would be completely beautiful and shining in God's eyes, as Nature and grace intended.

But we shouldn't worry about this, or at least only so much as our worry may help us grow. If we humbly take our concerns to our dear Mother, She will wash us with blood (the very fluid of life), making our souls soft and gentle, so that over time, we are healed and made beautiful, giving endless honor to Christ and joy to ourselves. Our Mother shall never cease her work in our lives till all Her children are born and brought forth into life. (I understood this in the showing where I saw the spiritual thirst, the love-longing that shall last until the end of time.)

In this way, our life is grounded in Jesus, our True Mother, in the foreseeing wisdom that has no beginning or end, along with the Father's high strength and the overarching unity of the Holy Spirit. When Christ took on human nature, we too were conceived into life; when He died on the Cross, He birthed us into endless life; and ever since and ever more, He feeds us and nurtures us, with a mother's gentle familiarity as she cares for her children's every intimate need.

Our Heavenly Mother is beautiful and sweet to our souls, and we are precious and lovely in Her sight; She sees our gentleness, beauty, and lovableness, all that any human mother sees in her children. Human children trust their mother's love; they love their mothers with humility and confidence, just as they love the other children in the family. Our Heavenly Mother is pleased by these same characteristics in Her children.

I believe that life offers us no higher roles than those we find in childhood, even though as children, our strength and intelligence were not fully developed yet. Only when we reach the Father's glad and friendly Presence will we climb again as high as we do in childhood, for then we shall truly understand what He meant when He said, "All shall be well, and you shall see for yourself that absolutely everything will be well." And then the joyous kindness of our Mother, in Christ, shall begin anew, a Divine joy whose beginning shall endure forever, a new beginning that never ends.

And in this way I understand that all God's children shall be birthed into natural life by the Divine Mother, and then by grace brought back again to God.

The Fifteenth Revelation

LXIV
You Shall Go Higher

Before going on to describe the next revelation, Julian admits here that she has faced depression and despair. What she is shown next takes its meaning from that admission. God has compassion on our sadness, our weariness, our spiritual inertia. We are not condemned for being this way, but instead we are accepted and loved. The implication is that we too should feel compassion and have patience with ourselves, knowing that regardless of our weakness, we "shall come higher," into the Divine Realm. This upward journey is not dependent on our own efforts (it will take place regardless of our lassitude and discouragement), nor is our inner reality clouded by our outer dullness.

Julian's image of a rotting dead body is one she would have seen in reality during Norwich's Plague years, a hideous and terrifying sight that contrasts sharply with her confidence in the eternal undimmed beauty of our deepest identities.

I used to long for God to deliver me from this world's life. I saw so clearly the sadness and sighing that is here, and I yearned for the wholeness and joy that is in the life to come. Even if the only pain in this world were the absence of our Protector, that sometimes seemed to me like more than I could bear. My life was filled with mourning, and I ached to know the world to come. My own wretchedness, laziness, and weakness seemed like burdens too heavy to bear.

In the midst of these feelings our considerate Protector answered me with these patient words of comfort: "Suddenly you shall be taken from all your pain, sickness, despair, and distress. You shall come higher, into My Realm, where I will be your reward, and you shall be filled with love and delight. And then you will never again feel any kind of pain; nothing will distress you; no sluggishness will weaken you. Joy and light will be yours endlessly. Knowing this waits for you, why should you be so upset about this world's temporary discomforts, since they are My will, My treasure?"

These words—"suddenly you shall be taken"—showed me that God rewards us for our patience as we abide in the Divine Will, and that our patience grows deeper the longer we live. Not knowing how long we will live is good for us, for if we knew exactly when we would leave this world, we would not need the patience we need now. God wills that while our souls dwell in our bodies, we always feel we are at the very point of leaving our bodies behind. For in truth, our entire life, all the weakness and dullness we experience here, is actually only a single point from which we shall step suddenly into such delight that all our pain will disappear into nothingness.

At this point in the vision, I saw a body lying on the ground, so decayed and rotten that it looked like a swollen heap of stinking manure. Suddenly, a small bright child leapt out of the body and glided up into heaven, fast and supple as a sunbeam, perfectly formed and lovely, as clean and new as a flower. The rotting body symbolizes our mortal flesh—but the small child shows the utter purity and wholeness of our inner selves. I found myself thinking: "I can see nothing of the child's loveliness in that decaying body—and I catch not even a whiff of the body's decay on the child."

It is a greater joy when we are taken from pain than when pain is taken from us—for pain that is taken away may return, but when we who live in love are taken from pain, we are filled with an overarching comfort and given a blissfully clear vision. In this Divine promise of deliverance I saw our Protector's amazing compassion for all our sighing and sadness. God wants us to be comforted by the promise of eternal joy, the total fulfillment that waits for us. I understood this when I heard these words: "You shall come higher, into My Realm, where I will be your reward, and you shall be filled with love and delight."

God wants us to focus our thoughts on this joyful concept as often as we can, for as long as we can, with the help of Divine grace; making space in our lives for these thoughts will bless our souls as they bless God. Eventually, when we fall back into our heaviness and spiritual blindness, our physical and spiritual pains, our weakness, God wants us to know we are never forgotten. That is what these words meant: "And then you will never again feel any kind of pain; nothing will distress you; no sluggishness will weaken you. Joy and bliss will be yours endlessly. Knowing this waits for you, why should you be so upset about this world's temporary discomforts, since they are My will, My treasure?"

Our Protector wants us to help ourselves with wide-open mouths to as much as we can of the comfort and direction God offers, focusing all our attention there—while at the same time, we only nibble at this world's troubles and discomforts before we set them aside as insignificant. The less we focus on them, the less important they will feel, and the less they will bother us—and the more gratitude and reward shall be ours in Heaven.

LXV
No Need to Worry

> As Julian nears the conclusion of her revelations, she emphasizes that by cultivating the perspective that God is in control here and now (not just in some far-off spiritual eternity), we will be less bothered by fears and worries. Julian is careful to say, though, that our feelings of distress never earn God's anger. Instead, her implication is that we make ourselves suffer needlessly when we lose sight of spiritual reality—and yet even in the midst of the needless anguish, "even in those times when we are in so much pain and distress that we cannot focus on anything but our feelings," writes Julian, "we can rest assured that these sensations count for nothing; we can pass over them lightly, without paying much attention to them."

When we commit ourselves to choosing God in this life, because we love God, we can be sure we are endlessly loved in return. This unconditional love works grace in our lives. God wants us to be as certain now of the joy that waits us in the world to come as we will be then, when we actually experience it. The more we rest in this certainty, with a gentle reverence, the more God is pleased.

The reverence I speak of here is a healthy, humble, and deferential awe of our Protector; in other words, we see how amazingly great is our Protector and how amazingly small we are. This sense of perspective gives us a strength God loves. It allows us to feel the Divine Presence in our lives, that Presence that is what we yearn for most, for it makes our faith strong and our hope certain. Such awe and reverence, when supported by great love, is a sweet and delicious nourishment for our souls.

God wants me to see myself as bound to the Divine in love now as if I had already been completely rescued and lifted into Heaven. This is how we should all think of our Divine Lover. What's more, God's love creates in us such a unity that we cannot separate ourselves from each other.

God showed me this so that our love will be increased, while our fears are diminished. For if we are filled with awe for the Divine, then we will not be impressed or overwhelmed by any other force. God wants us to see that all the Enemy's strength is locked up in our Friend's hand. That is why we have no reason to fear anything but God whom we love. All other fears are caused by our emotions, our physical condition, and our imagination.

That is why, even in those times when we are in so much pain and distress that we cannot focus on anything but our feelings, we can rest assured that these sensations count for nothing; we can pass over them lightly, without paying much attention to them. Why? Because God wants to be in an intimate relationship with us; and if we know God, love God, and are filled with reverence and awe for God, we shall have peace. Our minds will be at rest. Everything God does will create in our minds an enclosed garden of joy and delight, a place where we can be safe and happy. This is what our Protector showed me with these words: "Why should you be so upset about this world's temporary discomforts, since they are My will, My treasure?"

Now I have described the fifteen revelations that God gave to my mind. Over the years these visions have been renewed by new light, new touches—I trust from the same Spirit that originally showed them to me. The first showing began early in the morning, at about four o'clock, and they proceeded past me in a procession (like a wonderful parade) until a little after nine.

LXVI
The End of the Showings

> Here we catch a glimpse of Julian as someone who is very much like ourselves. As she comes to herself after her supernatural revelations, she dismisses them as delirium; when a monk takes them seriously, she is embarrassed and ashamed. For the first time, we sense that her thoughts are distorted by her fever. Her next revelation comes to her in a dream, and yet, Julian finds Divine meaning there as well.

And after this, on the following night, the good Protector showed me a sixteenth revelation, which was the conclusion and confirmation of the previous fifteen.

Before I describe that sixteenth showing, I need to tell you about my physical weakness and wretchedness. I said in the beginning that all my pain was taken suddenly from me, and this lasted through all fifteen revelations. As the fifteenth showing came to a close, however, my vision darkened. I knew then I was going to live, despite my mortal weakness, but soon after that, my sickness came over me again. First, my head began to pound and roar, and then all at once my entire body filled with sickness, just as it had been before the showings. Instantly, I felt as spiritually barren and dry as if I had never been comforted. I moaned and cried, overwhelmed by my physical pain and my emotional discomfort.

A monk came by and asked me how I was feeling. When I told him I had been delirious and raving, he laughed out loud with genuine amusement. I said, "I saw the Cross in front of me, and I thought it was bleeding." When I said this, his face became sober and full of awe. I was embarrassed by my careless words, and I thought to myself, This man is taking me seriously. So I said nothing more, but he spoke of what I had told him with such earnest reverence that I was ashamed. After he left, I cried, longing to confess to a priest—but at that time, I could not bring myself to tell a priest anything. I thought, No priest is going to believe me, when I don't even believe it myself.

You see, I believed the showings while they were taking place, and in the midst of the experience, I intended to always believe them—but like a fool, I let my intention fade from my mind. Look how pathetic I was! I separated myself from God, and I did myself and our Protector a great unkindness, all because I was feeling a little physical pain. As a result, I lost for a time the comfort the showings had given me from our Protector God. I'm telling you this so you will see what I am like.

But our thoughtful and considerate Protector did not leave me there in my foolishness. All day I lay quietly, trusting in God's mercy, and then I fell asleep.

At once, I dreamed the Fiend was at my throat. His face was pressed near mine, a visage like a young man's but so long and lean that it seemed distorted. I had never seen such a thing. It was brick red, freckled with black spots like the soot that falls on the hearth, and the matted locks that hung over his forehead were red as rust. He grinned at me slyly, flashing his white teeth, and I shuddered with horror. His hands were animal paws that clasped my throat as though he wanted to strangle me if only he could.

Unlike the other showings, which took place while I was awake, this horrible vision came to me while I slept. But even while I dreamed, I trusted that God's mercy would rescue me—and our loving Protector gave me the grace to wake up then.

I felt as though I were dying. The people who were sitting with me leaned over me and put damp cloths on my forehead. I began to relax, but then I saw smoke drifting in the door. I could feel the heat beating in at us, and I breathed a foul odor. "God bless us!" I cried. "Everything's on fire!" I thought it was an actual fire that would burn us all to death.

"Don't you smell the stench?" I asked those who were with me.

"No," they said. They didn't feel anything.

"Blessed be God!" I said, for I knew then that this was the Fiend again, come to disturb me. This time I turned to all the Protector had shown me, supported by the faith of the Church (for I saw my visions and the Church's teachings as one thing), and I clung to the showings for comfort. After a while, the vision of the Fiend faded away, and I sank into a deep peaceful rest. This time, no sickness bothered my body, and my sense of myself was quiet and unafraid.

The Sixteenth Revelation

LXVII
Jesus Makes His Home in Our Souls

Julian indicates here the meaning of her last revelation: that the Second Person of the Trinity and the human soul are intimately, permanently connected (without beginning or end). The Divine is at home in the human mind, and that dwelling place can never be removed.

In Julian's original, she speaks of the "harte" as the place where both Jesus and her own soul dwell. Modern-day Christians are also accustomed to thinking of their hearts as Christ's dwelling place, but when we use the word "heart" today, do we truly know what we mean? We know we are not talking about the physical organ that pumps blood through our bodies, but we do not know where the heart of which we speak is located instead, and we cannot describe its substance. Are our hearts the same as our souls? We're not sure.

As a result, any time we refer to the "heart," we throw our discussion into the vague realm of the spiritual and the emotional, somewhere distinctly different from the concrete specifics of the physical world. Our ambiguous usage of the word allows us to draw a dividing line through our concept of reality: on one side lies the physical, observable world of science and the body; on the other side floats a hazy spiritual world filled with emotions and perceptions that cannot be tied to the opposite side of the dividing line. Most of us manage to believe in both sides at once, while at the same time finding few occasions to draw tangible connections between them. By doing so, we make any conversations between science and theology, as well as between psychiatry and spirituality, difficult to have, if not impossible, since we are talking about two non-intersecting realities. We "feel with our hearts," according to the language of the one reality, while we "perceive with our brains" in the language we use on the other side. We speak of our hearts and minds as two different and often contrary aspects of our natures (despite the fact that psychiatry tells us that both emotions and thoughts take place physically within the neurons and other cells of our bodies).

When Julian spoke of her "harte," however, she used the word to mean the center of her being, the focal place of her identity within her body. The medieval concept of heart was more closely connected to memory than to emotions, and "harte" and "minde" were often used interchangeably as having to do with the intellect and our power to think and remember.

Because of this, I chose in many cases to use the word "mind" instead of "heart" in my translation of Julian's writing. Doing so is consistent with Julian's insistence that our physical beings and our spiritual are meant to be a united identity, functioning in a single world—and that no dividing line was ever drawn by God between the physical realm and the spiritual.

And then our Protector opened my spiritual eyes and showed me my soul in the middle of my mind. The soul was large, an endless world, a kingdom of delight, a city of great worth. In the center of the city sat our Protector Jesus, both God and Human, a tall, beautiful Person, highest Watcher over the realm, most joyous and solemn King, worthiest Protector, clad in glory. He deserves His position in the soul, a position that leads straight to peace and rest.

The Divine Essence—greatest strength, highest wisdom, deepest unity and sweetness—effortlessly guides Heaven and Earth and all that is, and makes everything bud with life. But the place that Jesus takes in our souls is unique, inviolable; it can never be removed. He finds in us His most comfortable home, His endless dwelling place.

I saw in this vision the satisfaction and fulfillment Christ finds in the human soul. God the Creator, God the Child, and God the Holy Spirit all worked to create humanity's soul, and it was created perfectly. The Trinity takes endless joy in the human soul, for the Divine knows that which best suits God, and the human soul suits God endlessly and without beginning.

All that the Divine has made shows God's Protection. I understood this by seeing the image of a small creature who looked up at its mistress, awed by how great she was and how wonderful was everything about her. And after the little creature had seen all this, it was never happy living anywhere but close to its mistress. This image showed me that our souls can never be at rest so long as they seek their comfort from things whose value is less than their own. The self is higher than all Creation, and yet we can never see our selves for very long; instead, when we look at our selves, we see the Divine, our Creator, living within us. For in the human soul is God's truest dwelling place. The light that shines from the City of the Self is the splendor of our Protector's love.

And what makes us enjoy the Divine more than to see the joy God takes in human beings? For I saw in this same vision that if the human soul had been made better, more lovely, or more noble than it was, it would not have pleased God as much. We are made exactly as God wants us to be. We only need to lift our minds above Earth's empty sorrows so that we can rejoice in the Divine joy.

LXVIII
Overcoming Troubles

> Here at last is the conclusion of Julian's long hours of revelation, summed up in her final statement: "For Christ did not say, 'You'll never encounter storms, you'll never have troubles, you'll never be afflicted.' What He said was, 'You shall not be overcome.'"
>
> And all shall be well.

This was a delightful vision, and the joy and peace it offered never ends. Dwelling on this vision while we live in this world pleases God, and it is good for us. The soul that looks at God becomes like God, and is united with God's rest and peace. I felt an unusual joy and happiness when I saw that Jesus was *sitting* in my vision, for His position implied to me a quiet security, an endless dwelling.

And through this sight God gave me a firm knowledge of the truth of all I had seen in the earlier showings (for since Jesus lives within me, it is His authority I claim). When I had paid close attention to this, then our good Protector spoke gently to me without any voice, just as before: "Know now that you were not delirious when you saw these revelations. Take them and believe them. Keep yourself within all I have showed you. Take comfort from it, and trust it—and you shall not be overcome."

These last words assured me that our Protector Jesus was truly the One who had shown me all I had seen in the visions. The first time He spoke in the showings, He said, "This is the way the devil was overcome" (referring to His own joyful Endurance on the Cross), and in the same way, His last words assured us all that we are truly safe: "You shall not be overcome."

All the teaching I received through the showings was meant for all of us, not just for me. God wants all Christ-followers to know what was revealed in the visions. The phrase, "You shall not be overcome," was said with such decisiveness and strength, so that in all the trials and troubles that come our way, we can find comfort and assurance. For Christ did not say, "You'll never encounter storms, you'll never have troubles, you'll never be afflicted." What He said was, "You shall not be overcome." God wants us to pay attention to these words, so that we can be strong in our trust, in the midst of sadness as much as in the midst of well-being.

For God loves and enjoys us—and the Divine Will wants us to love and enjoy God in return, and rest in this strength.

And all shall be well.

Soon after this, the showings came to a close and I saw no more.

LXIX
Saved from the Enemy

> In these "epilogue" chapters (Julian's descriptions of what came after her visions), we see her again in a delirious state, yet still clinging to her faith in God.

After this, the Fiend returned with his heat and stench, so that I became preoccupied with anxiety. The stench was so vile that it was painful. I heard a gabbling, like two people jabbering insults at each other at the same time, as though they were in the midst of an argument, but their voices were only mutters, too soft for me to understand. Despair moved inside me, though, and it seemed to me that the voices were pretending to recite prayers, the kind of prayers that are said loudly with the mouth while the mind and spirit pay no heed, as though they were mocking my faith.

But our Protector God gave me a strong dose of grace, so that I was filled with trust. I spoke words of comfort out loud to myself, the way I would have spoken to another person who was in similar trouble. I realized that when our thoughts are too busy it is not the same as when our bodies are busy, and so, as I set my physical eyes on the Cross that had given me so much comfort earlier, I occupied my tongue with repeating the story of Christ's Endurance and the faith of the Holy Church, and I fastened my mind on God with all my confidence and strength. I thought to myself, "Now your mind is preoccupied with your Faith, so that you will not be overcome by your Enemy. If you could keep your thoughts busy like this forever, so that you had no time for any separation from God to creep into your mind, that would indeed be a valuable occupation!" I realized that when I do not separate my thoughts from God, I am completely safe from all the fiends of Hell, all the enemies of my soul.

And in this way the night passed, until it was about six in the morning, when at last the voices ceased, leaving nothing but the stench lingering awhile in the air. I laughed, for I knew the strength of Christ's Endurance had delivered me, just as our Protector Jesus Christ had said it would.

LXX
We Rely on Faith

For the remainder of her book, Julian continues to analyze and "unfold" the meaning of the visions she experienced. She explains here that moments of deep spiritual awareness are not our "normal" state of being, nor will they ever be. That is why we rely on faith.

The word "faith" first took on a religious connotation at some point during Julian's lifetime. Up until then, "belief" had been the word reserved for religious experiences, meaning "trust in God," while "faith" was used for human relationships, in the sense of "loyalty based upon a promise." "Faith" had evolved from the same ancient roots as "bide," which carried within it the implication of staying, enduring a wait, continuing, relying. All these shades of meaning would have still been inherent in the word Julian used.

Today, when we say we "keep faith" in our human relationships, we mean we remain committed, in good times and bad, whether the person makes us furious or makes us laugh out loud with delight. If we apply that same sense of enduring commitment—the willingness to wait out the bad times—to our relationship to God, we have a better understanding of the faith Julian describes here.

ALL SHALL BE WELL

Throughout the entire vision I had experienced, our good Protector let me know these intense perceptions would not last: I would need to rely on faith to keep the showings alive. The vision left behind no sign nor token to prove its truth, only God's word that I should believe it. And so I do.

I believe these showings came from the One who rescued us, that they are consistent with the entire Faith, and so I believe with joy all I was shown. I have tied my life to these visions with the words Christ spoke to me next: "Keep yourself within all I have showed you. Take comfort from it, and trust it."

And so I am compelled to make all I was shown a constant part of my faith. For on the day of the showings, after they were over, like a miserable outcast I forsook what I had seen and told people I'd merely been delirious with fever. Our Protector Jesus was kind enough that He did not let the vision disappear but instead He showed it to me again yet more fully within my soul, with the holy light of His love, saying with such tender strength, "Be sure of this, what you saw today was no hallucination." It was as though He were saying to me, "You don't have the ability to hold on to the kind of vision you experienced during the showings, so pay close attention now to what I've shown you, so that you'll remember." This message was not meant only for that day but for my entire life, so that my faith would be rooted in the words He said next: "Keep yourself within all I have shown you. Take comfort from it, and trust it—and you shall not be overcome."

When He said this, He meant that we should fasten all He had shown me to our minds, so that it lives with us until we die—and after our deaths, it will be made complete in the joy we know then. Knowing that Christ is whole and sweet, we can trust His promise.

WE RELY ON FAITH

So many things oppose our faith—our own blindness and the spiritual enemies that lurk both within us and outside us—but our Lover sheds light on our spiritual eyes and teaches us both from within our own minds and from the circumstances of our external lives, so that we may know God. The Divine teaches us in many ways, but whatever the way, we are to open our eyes and our minds. Life's sweetness and unity reaches no higher than faith, and we will find no help for our souls that lies below faith. Only in faith can we live within our Protector's safety. His own strength, the function of who Christ is, keeps us there, and we are made strong even in the midst of spiritual battles. Without these battles, our faith would mean little and would merit no reward.

LXXI
Our Protector's Face

> The word Julian used for "face" is *cheer*, which in the fourteenth century had a far different meaning than it does today. Julian would have connected the concept of "cheer" (face) with "mood, demeanor," but clearly, for her it also had to do with identity—our inner identity (or face) versus our outer.
>
> As Julian discusses Christ's face, she is speaking of the Divine expressions we are capable of perceiving. Christianity has often emphasized the first two expressions—sad endurance and tender compassion—but Julian's perception of Christ's expressions of "joyous kindness" and "glad friendliness" is unique. This is a Divine expression that Christianity seems to have overlooked all too often.

Glad and sweet is our Protector's face. Christ is always looking at us; our souls are constantly held in His loving, yearning gaze, for He longs for our faces to look back at Him. When we do, I hope Christ's grace shall draw out our inner faces so that they become one with our outer faces, unified with God and with each other, in the true and eternal joy that is Jesus.

I have three ways of thinking about our Protector's face. The first is His expression of endurance, as He showed it in this life while He was dying on the Cross. Although this expression is sad and troubled, at the same time it shines with joy, for Christ is God. The second expression is one of empathy and compassion, which He reveals to anyone who needs His mercy. The third is one of joyous kindness, a glad friendliness that shall never end, and this is the expression I see most often.

When we are hurting and sad, we see Christ's face as it looked while He hung dying from the Cross, and His strength helps us bear our own suffering. When we feel separated from God, Christ's expression of empathy and compassion keeps us safe and defends us against all our enemies. In this life, these are the two expressions we may see most, but they are always mingled with the third, His joyful friendliness, which is the one we shall see most fully in Heaven.

Our lives here on Earth are filled with touches of grace and glimpses of Divine light, which guide our faith on paths of hope and love, commitment and repentance. As we make a space in our lives for looking at God, we will experience all manner of comfort and happiness.

LXXII
Meddling with Sin Clouds Our Vision

Here Julian describes three valid modes of human perception: knowing God, knowing our own selves, and knowing our separation from God. Julian acknowledges the reality of the anguish caused by this sense of separation, even as she insists that in God's sight we are never separated. Sin is what hides true reality from us, but it has no power to damage or diminish that reality—and the suffering it causes makes us more aware of how much we long for God.

In Julian's later versions of her revelation, she added the additional comments I included here in this chapter's final five paragraphs. In these lines, she struggles still further with sin and human identity, and ultimately concludes that the "sinner"—the Exiled One—is nothing. It has no substance. All that is real in us is united with God. If we could somehow extract the "sinner" from any human being, we would find that what remained was not a small, diminished sliver of a person but a person who was truly whole, one with God.

We can choose to align our awareness with our blindness, focusing on the shadowy, illusory world of exile—and when we do, we experience the anguish that is so common in this life. Or, says Julian, we can allow this same sense of separation from God to be the impetus that drives us ever closer to the Divine.

MEDDLING WITH SIN CLOUDS OUR VISION

But I need to explain now how I understood sin to be deadly, and yet it does not kill the creatures it effects, for they live in God's joy forever.

I saw that two opposing things can never exist in one place, and these are the most opposite that two things can be, the highest joy and the deepest pain. The highest joy is being in the Divine Presence, clearly, endlessly, seeing God, feeling God, filled with perfect and complete joy. This was the glad, friendly face our Protector showed me in the second showing, where I understood that sin is on the furthest opposite end from all that is God, and so long as we meddle with anything remotely connected to sin (as long as we allow our awareness to be mixed together with that which separates us from an awareness of God), we shall never see clearly our Protector's joyful and kind face.

The more horrible and painful our sins, the deeper we are hidden from this glad sight. This is why we feel so often as though we are in mortal danger, as though we were in a region of Hell, but it is only the sorrow and pain within our own minds that we feel. But we are like dead people, unable to see the reality of our own joyous life. And yet we are not dead in God's sight nor does the Divine Presence ever leave us. God's joy in us will never be complete, though, until we finally see clearly God's friendly, loving face. This is what we were made for, this is the fulfillment of our deepest natures, and grace brings us to what we were always meant to be. And this is the way that sin is deadly, but only for a short time in our lives' endless blessing.

The more glimpses we get by grace of God's happy love, the more we long to see it in all its fullness. For even though our Protector God dwells in us and is here with us, even though God clasps us close and encloses us with gentle love and never leaves us and is nearer to us than tongue can tell or mind can think—yet our yearning and sorrow will never end until we at last see clearly the Divine Face in all its friendliness and joy. When we see that glad sight, we will no more sigh and sorrow. We know that all is whole, each good thing in our lives solid and unshaken.

In this I saw both reason for laughter and reason for tears. I laughed because our Protector, our Maker, is so near to us, in us, and we are in God, kept completely safe by the sweet unity of the Divine—and I cried because our spiritual eyes are so blind, and we are so weighed down by our mortal flesh and the darkness of sin that we cannot see clearly the kind and happy face of our Protector God. And because our eyes are so dim, we can scarcely believe or trust in God's great love and our own utter safety. That is why our lives are filled with tears, especially spiritually. For the very nature of our souls makes us constantly yearn with a sense of emptiness; even if everything comforting and good God had ever made in either Heaven or Earth were given to us, we would still be filled with spiritual sorrow if we did not see God's glad face. And if we were in the midst of life's most terrible pain and sorrow and we saw God's face, the pain would not trouble us.

The sight of God's face ends all spiritual pain; it fulfills all joys; it completes every kindness. God showed me this with these words: "I am highest; I am lowest; I am all." We have three ways of knowing reality: first, we know our Protector God; second, we know our own selves, as both Nature and Divine Grace created us; and third, we know humility because we see our souls alongside our weakness and sin. As best I can understand, the showings were given to me so that we could better understand these three modes of perception.

Oh Exiled One, separated from God and from your own sense of yourself! What are you? You are nothing. When I saw that God had made all things, I saw no sinners such as you. And when I saw that God is in all things, I did not see you. And when I saw that God does all things, both small and large, I did not see you. And when I saw our Protector Jesus in our souls—sharing His worth with us, His love, His pleasure, His authority, and all that He has made—I did not see you. And that is why I am certain that you are truly nothing. Anything that has to do with you in any way is nothing, and it shall be endlessly and totally overthrown. May God shield us from you! Let it be so in love.

God has shown me that sin is exile and separation from God. This separation is in all things that are not in unity with God. It is the spiritual blindness into which we fell when humanity first sinned, and from that follows all exile, all pain, and all miseries both spiritual and physical. From it also follows all that is on the Earth or anywhere else that is not unified with God.

So now we ask: What are we humans? And here is my answer: if everything in us that was not united with God was taken away, we would be completely whole. When our state of exile is taken away, then all that is left is our union with the Divine. Humans and God are one.

What is it in this life that separates us into two? Is it evil? Or is it good? And I say, in that it serves us and helps us grow, it is good (it heals us and unites us with God)—but in that it makes us lose our sense of who we are in the Divine, it is evil. If we willfully point our minds toward this state of exile, then it is sin—and we are plunged into a state of suffering that is worse than all others. But if we hate our feelings of exile and separation from the Divine, when we are filled with love and yearning for God, then we are fine. When we sincerely feel these things, we may sin because we are weak or blind, but we still do not fall, because we will rise up again in strength and see God anew.

We were created for love, and God constantly loves us and longs for our love in return. And when we love Jesus with all our physical strength and mental awareness, we are at peace.

LXXIII
Soul Sickness Comes in Two Forms

Having affirmed that sin has no ultimate power to touch reality, Julian next asserts that we should expand our definition of sin to cover despair and self-doubt, since these hide the Divine Face from our sight as effectively as does any other dishonesty we indulge.

In this chapter, Julian also speaks of our human tendency to trust that God is all-wise, and all-powerful—but to doubt that the Divine is also all-love, far surpassing any human ability to love.

Here (and in many other chapters), Julian's original text uses the word "like": Jesus "liked" his sacrifice on the cross; God wants us to "like" Divine Love. Our modern usage of the word makes these statements seem to be extreme understatements. In the language we speak today, "love" has become the superlative of "like."

But today's understanding of these words has in some way diminished them. In Julian's day the phrase "I like it" was still in the process of evolving from its original "It likes me." In modern Spanish, the construction is the same: *"Tu me gustas"* (I like you) means literally, "You please me," "You give me pleasure." For Julian, "like" had to do with the feelings of delight and satisfaction we feel in response to something. The original, deepest meanings of "love" were quite different; they had to do with a willingness to take action on another's behalf, to care about another's well-being.

What Julian makes clear is this: God both loves us and likes us. Loving and liking are the two hands that draw us to God. On the one hand, through Jesus, the Divine Heart gave everything for our well-being; this active, ongoing love is the foundation of the very universe. But on the other hand, we give God pleasure; God delights in the relationship humans have with the Divine. In the same way, we give ourselves to God—and in return, we are pleased beyond measure.

Our Protector showed me these teachings in three ways: through my physical sight, through my thoughts, and through spiritual vision. I have described the physical sights I saw as exactly as I can, and I have repeated my thoughts just as our Protector put them in my mind, but I will never be able to fully describe the spiritual vision. And yet I am inspired to try to write more on this topic, as God gives me grace.

Spiritually, I perceived that sin bothers us most in two forms—despair and self-doubt—which are what cause us the most trouble and pain. God wants to heal this soul sickness in our minds.

SOUL SICKNESS COMES IN TWO FORMS

I am speaking now of people who want to do God's will and yet still experience spiritual blindness and physical inertia. We do not see these qualities as sin—something that separates us from God—and yet they are. God wants us to see them in this light, so that we shun them just as we do all other sin.

This is why our Protector revealed His patience through His long Endurance on the Cross, and the joy and satisfaction that Endurance gave Him because of His love. He wants us to take hope and inspiration from His experience, so that we too will gladly and wisely bear our troubles. When we do so, we give God pleasure and we help our own souls endlessly.

We go through so much pain in life because we do not fully comprehend love. The Trinity's three Persons—Strength, Wisdom, and Love—are all equally present in the human self, but my mind can best understand love. I believe God wants that we see and enjoy all life in the light of love. But we are ignorant and blind when it comes to this realization. Some of us believe that God is Almighty, able to do all things, and many of us believe God is All-Wisdom, able to do all things. But we stop short at believing that God is All-Love, able to do all things. This ignorance on our part is what hinders us most, I believe.

When we come to God through the Church, we learn to hate sin. We look back on our past sins with guilt and sorrow, and yet we continue to fall away from our promises over and over in small daily ways, failing to live in the new state of being our Protector has created for us. Then we are filled with shame and sorrow; the sight of our selves weighs us down, to the point that we can scarcely find any comfort.

We mistake this fear and guilt for humility, but it is not; it is instead a sick and ugly blindness, a weakness. We do not realize that these feelings are sin. The Enemy sends them creeping into our minds so subtly that we do not know enough to reject them the way we would other sins. They are lies, sent by the one who hates our souls.

Of all the Trinity's friendly joys, God wants most for us to know the sureness of love. Only love will give us comfort, for love allows us to see the gentleness of Divine strength and wisdom. If God can forgive our sins, why shouldn't we forgive ourselves? We do not need to be weighed down with fear and doubt and shame.

LXXIV
No Fear Pleases God Except the Awe of God

The word Julian uses here for "fear" was actually "dread," a word that had to do with avoiding something negative. Julian indicates that this feeling can impel us to seek God (allowing what is negative and destructive to be transformed into something positive and creative, which, as Julian has asserted again and again, is a recurring Divine quality). When our fear turns into doubt in God's goodness, however, it becomes most destructive. "Doubt" stemmed from the concept of "being of two minds" (double-minded). To be of two minds about God's goodness and love is to make ourselves vulnerable to despair, the loss of hope (the ability to look forward in anticipation). In other words, we become stuck, unable to see the reality beyond our present circumstance.

Awe, however, is a different kind of fear. Julian's fourteenth-century word had recently come from the same roots as "wary" and "aware." It meant "to be alert, to be attentive, to take heed." Awe in this sense is closely tied to love, insists Julian, for both have to do with responsive awareness. "Though God can transform all our fears," concludes Julian, "be careful of any fear that makes you feel separated from the Divine. The only sort of fear that is truly of God is the fear that makes us flee to our

> Protector's breast, throwing our whole selves on God the way a child buries his head in his mother."
>
> In Julian's original, she uses the word "wrong" to describe all other kinds of fear. In her day, wrongness meant crookedness, in the same way that rightness had to do with straightness. The sense of "bad, immoral" in connection with the word was only just developing. As we think of wrong in terms of distortion, twistedness, and crookedness, we may gain deeper insight than we can from the simplistic word "bad."

I understood that fear comes in four forms.

First is the fear that overcomes us suddenly when we feel we are vulnerable to danger. This fear can do us good, because it purges us of our selfishness, the way physical illness or other distress can also purify us. If we patiently endure these sorts of pain, they can help us grow.

The second sort of fear is the fear of pain. This can wake us out of sin's sleep. When we are asleep, we cannot perceive the Holy Spirit's gentle comfort, so we need to be shaken awake. We may fear physical death or spiritual enemies—but if this fear moves us to seek God's comfort and mercy, it can become a door through which we feel the Spirit's friendly breath blowing us into repentance.

The third fear is that of doubt, the dread that causes us to despair. God hates despair. The Divine longs to transform this feeling in our hearts into a knowledge of love, and grace will do so if we rest in the knowledge that we were created for love. Our Protector is never pleased when we doubt that God is good.

The fourth fear is that of awe, a deep reverence for God—and this is the only fear that truly pleases God. This is a gentle fear. The more we experience it, the less we feel it, for as we gaze at God, we are overcome with love's sweetness.

This awe-fear is the only form of fear that is love's brother. Both are rooted in us by our Maker's sweet unity, and they shall never be taken from us. We experience love both by our innate nature and by grace. The Divine Protectorship, the Fatherhood of God, fills us with awe, even as the Divine Goodness, the Motherhood of God, fills us with love. This awe-fear cannot be separated from love, and yet they are two separate forces at work in our souls, though neither can be had without the other. That is why the one who loves also has awe and reverence, though she may not be aware of the awe so much as the love.

We should be on our guard against any fear other than this awe-fear. Though God can transform all our fears, be careful of any fear that makes you feel separated from the Divine. The only sort of fear that is truly of God is the fear that makes us flee to our Protector's breast, throwing our whole selves on God the way a child buries his head in his mother. This fears makes us aware that we are weak and needy, but only so that we are driven to God's everlasting sweetness and unity, to the friendly Divine love.

The sort of fear that makes us cling to God, full of trust and confidence, is the only type of fear that is good and true, springing from grace. Fear that does not possess these qualities is a crooked sort of thing that pulls us out of alignment. Recognize the difference and refuse to allow anything that distorts the truth to take root in your mind.

The awe of God comes from the Spirit's gentle action, the same movement that lives in Heaven in the Divine Presence; it is kind, humble, with the delicious taste of love. Love makes us intimate with God; awe gives us humility; and both are equal.

We should ask our Protector God to fill us with reverent love, gentle fear, and tenacious trust—for when we have both love and awe, our trust is always strong. The more we trust, the more love and worship we give to our Protector. And if our awe and love fail (God forbid!), then our trust is diminished. That is why we pray that our Protector's grace will grant us this reverent love and gentle awe, Divine gifts that fill our minds and work. Without these, we cannot please God.

LXXV
Awe Is Heaven's Courtesy

> In this chapter, Julian further explains her concept of awe, linking it to the longing we feel for God (what she often refers to as "thirst"). Her description of the Last Day's trembling joy are in sharp contrast to the scenes of terror and doom that were common in her day.

God can do all that we need. And these are the three Divine qualities we need: love, longing, and compassion. God's loving compassion keeps us always safe, and God's longing draws us up into Heaven. The Divine thirst yearns to have all humanity united with God. This is the thirst that drew the holy ones who now live in Heaven's joy; God draws and drinks from the living members of the Divine Body, and yet God's thirst and longing never ends.

I saw three forms of Divine longing, all aimed at the same goal, and we have these same three forms of longing in ourselves as well, with the same power for good focused on the same endpoint. The first longing is for God to teach us to know and love the Divine forever; this makes our lives easier and directs us on our spiritual journeys. The second longing is for us to join God in Heaven's joy, where we will be taken out of all pain. The third longing is to make us complete in the Divine, totally satisfied and whole, and this shall happen on the Last Day, when our lives will be forever fulfilled at last. Our Faith has always told us that when God saves us, all our pain and sorrow shall end. And not only will we receive the same friendly joy that other souls have experienced in Heaven, but we will also receive a new, unique delight all our own, which will flow without limit from God into us, filling us full. This is the heavenly merchandise God planned to give us from the beginning, the treasure God keeps hidden for us, waiting until the time when we are increased enough to be able to receive it.

And as we are made complete, we shall see the true cause of all things God has done, the reason behind all our Protector suffered. And our joy and fulfillment shall be so deep, so high, so full of marvelous wonder, that we will be overwhelmed with reverent awe to the point that the very pillars of heaven will tremble and quake. But this form of trembling awe holds no pain; it is only the trembling of humble joy as we marvel at the greatness of our Maker compared to the littleness of all that is made. Perceiving this fills us with gentle humility.

This is what God wants us to understand by grace—and it is our very nature as well to yearn for this awareness and process in our lives, for it leads us on a straight road to God, it keeps us rooted in true life, and it unites us with the Divine. As good as God is, so great is God; as loveable as God is, so awe-inspiring is God.

Reverent awe is Heaven's courtesy. Just as we shall love and know God so much more in Heaven than we do now, we shall also be filled so much more with awe and reverence for the Divine greatness. And that is why all Heaven and Earth shall tremble before God.

LXXVI
Separation from God Is the Only Hell

Most of us have had the experience of hearing words much like these within our minds: "See what a wretched being you are, how bad you are, how unfaithful you are. You don't keep your promises. You tell Jesus you will do better, but you never do. You make the same mistakes over and over. Most of all, you're lazy and you waste time." But Julian insists that the attitude expressed in these phrases is destructive; it is an enemy of our soul's health; and it throws us into what she claims is the most painful hell we will ever experience: separation from our awareness of God's love.

Julian also reminds us not to focus our attention on others' sins. Compassion for others, she writes, is our protection against falling into sin ourselves.

I don't want to focus too much on this reverent awe, for I don't want to be misunderstood. Still, our Protector made clear to me that all souls are meant to feel awe in God's presence. But those souls who are lead by the Holy Spirit hate being separated from God far more than they fear any other concept of Hell. To my mind, the soul who is focused on the Divine Nature of our Protector Jesus hates no hell but that which comes when we separate ourselves from God. This is why God wants us to recognize sin (anything that comes between our eyes and God), so that we can pray and work and seek direction to avoid it—and if we do fall into sin, that we recover our footing promptly. Separating ourselves from God is the most pain we will ever experience.

We should not focus on others' sins either. Thinking about sin, whether our own or another's, creates a spiritual fog that robs from us the sight of God's beauty. Instead, we should seek God's healing and strength on behalf of us all, and when we look at another who has fallen into sin, we should focus only on compassion and our own brokenness, longing for God's healing for us both. Without this attitude, our own souls will trip and stumble into sin. Compassion is our protection.

In the showing given me by our Protector, I understood two opposing things: first, the greatest wisdom we can achieve, and second, the deepest foolishness. The greatest wisdom is for us to seek the will and guidance of our deepest and best Friend—Jesus. He guides us to hold tight to Him, to fasten ourselves to Him in the most intimate way possible, forever, in whatever condition we find ourselves, whether we are clean or dirty in our own eyes, for His love for us never changes. Whether we are well or ill, whole or broken, He wants us to never run away from Him. Because we are changeable while we live in this temporary life, we fall often into sin—and then the Enemy as well as our own foolishness and blindness fill us with fear and doubt by telling us, "See what a wretched being you are, how bad you are, how unfaithful you are. You don't keep your promises. You tell Jesus you will do better, but you never do. You make the same mistakes over and over. Most of all, you're lazy and you waste time."

This is how sin begins; this is how we who have committed ourselves to serving our Protector Jesus and focusing on His goodness are separated from Him. This separation is what makes us afraid to come into His gentle Presence. It is our Enemy's goal to thrust us backward with false fear, playing on our weakness. The Enemy wants to make us so burdened and exhausted with self-doubt and despair that we lose sight of our Everlasting Friend.

LXXVII
Don't Blame Yourself!

> This chapter speaks of Divine discipline, what Julian called "chastisement." Many of us connect discipline with spankings, and chastisement with scolding, but Julian takes pains to show that God's discipline is not punishment for our sins. (In the fourteenth century, "to chastise" meant simply "to purify"; again, we see our modern language's tendency to focus on negative meanings versus the frequently more positive implications of Middle English.) The ordinary challenges of mortal life itself, claims Julian, are the only penance God asks us to endure.
>
> At the end of this chapter, Julian again affirms the connection between courtesy and intimacy, this time directing us to follow God's example of respectful familiarity.

Our good Protector showed me the Fiend's hatred so I would understand that our Enemy causes anything that falls outside love and peace. Our weakness and foolishness trip us, but the Spirit's mercy and grace lifts us to even greater joy. Even if our Enemy wins something in our failures (for this is his business), he loses far more when we rise up anew. Because he hates us, our rising into our brightest essence is such a sorrow and pain for him that envy makes him continually burn. The sorrow he plans for us turns backward onto himself. Our Protector has cut off the Enemy's horns; when I saw this, I couldn't help but laugh out loud.

When we become aware that we are broken and exiled, we flee to our Protector—and in our flight, we are healed. For the more needy we are, the more we need to touch the hem of the Divine Presence. We should say to ourselves, "I know I have this pain inside me—but our Protector is All-Strong, with the strength to mend me; our Protector is All-Wisdom, with the insight to guide me; and our Protector is All-Good and loves me tenderly." We need to keep this perspective, for humility allows us to gladly yield to the Spirit's mercy and grace as our Protector makes us pure. This discipline will be light and comfortable so long as we keep ourselves satisfied with God and all the Divine works.

I did not see any of the self-punishments we take on ourselves, at least not specifically. What I received instead was a special, deep, and lovely insight into God's discipline, which comes to us as we keep in mind Christ's Endurance on the Cross. (For when we focus our thoughts on His Endurance, then we suffer it with Him, just as His friends did who were there to see it in person. This was shown to me in the thirteenth showing, near the beginning, where it spoke of compassion.) Christ says to us, "Don't accuse yourself. Don't worry that your tribulations and troubles are your own fault. I don't want you to be weighed down with sorrow for no real reason. Whatever you do, no matter how good you are, you will have troubles in this life. They are not punishments—but you can use them to turn your mind toward Me, so that your entire life is worthwhile and accomplishes something."

The world where we live is our prison, and this life is our penance—but as we are freed and healed, God wants us to take joy. We are healed because our Protector is with us, keeping us safe, leading us into joyful fulfillment. This is our Protector's endless joy: that He shall be our most intimate pleasure in Heaven, and our Protector and Keeper while we are here in this life. Our path and our Heaven are true love and sure trust. (He showed me this in all the showings, especially in the showing of His Endurance, where I chose Christ to be my Heaven.)

When we run to our Protector, we shall be comforted; when we touch God, we shall be made clean; when we cling to Christ, we will be free from fear and safe from all danger.

Our lovely Protector wants us to be as familiar with God as mind may think or soul desire. But let us not use our familiarity with recklessness, taking leave of respect. For Protector Christ is Himself the most familiar of all friends, and yet He is as respectful as He is familiar. And if we want to be in Heaven with Him forever, then we will become like Him in all things. To become perfectly like our Protector is to find our truest salvation and joy.

And if we don't know how to achieve this, why then, all we have to do is ask God to teach us—for that is the Divine pleasure, that is what brings God worth. Happy may God be!

LXXVIII
Even as We Are Lifted Up, Yet We Are Humbled

> We should not think that Julian ever intends to trivialize or dismiss the problem of evil. Her discussion here indicates how seriously she takes sin; she insists that God protects us from ever seeing just how truly hideous our sin is because the sight would be too terrible for us to bear.

In mercy, our Protector reveals our sin and weakness by the sweet, generous light of Christ Himself. Our sin is so vile and horrible that He is too kind to let us see it except by the light of His own mercy and grace. Because of this, Jesus wants us to understand four things: First, that He Himself is our ground, the soil from which we grow, the foundation on which we are built. Second, that He guards us and keeps us safe when we are in the midst of sin, when our own choices allow our enemies to surround us, when we do not even realize our own need. Third, that He guards us with care and kindness, showing us where we have gone astray. And fourth, that His presence is always with us, and His loving gaze never wavers, for He wants us to turn back to Him and become united with Him in love, as He is with us.

When we understand this, we can look at our sin and not despair. In fact, we need to see our sin clearly, so that we can lose our false pride and presumption, so that we understand how we have become bent from the shape God wanted for us. As our Protector shows us the smallest glimpses of this reality, we are able to throw ourselves forward toward the reality we cannot see. God is kind; we only see that which we can bear to see. This gentle revelation of reality allows us to be broken from all that is not God—and then our Rescuer shall heal us and make us whole, at one with the Divine.

An ongoing breaking and healing is intended for all humanity during this life. The person who is nearest to God often sees her own sin most clearly, allowing it to unite her with me; and I who am the lowest and smallest am comforted by being joined with she who is so high, for our Protector has made us one in love. (This was revealed to me in the showing I described in chapter XXXVII, but at the time, I was experiencing so much joy simply looking at Jesus that I didn't pay attention; so our courteous Protector did not teach me further at the time until I received the grace and focus to comprehend.)

When we set aside a space for God in our minds and lives, we may be lifted up through our Protector's gift of kindness—but yet we still need to be aware of our sin and weakness. Without this awareness, we will not be truly humble, and without humility, we cannot be rescued. We cannot gain this awareness through our own strength, however, nor through the messages sent to our minds by our spiritual enemies. If our enemies had their way, we would never gain this understanding until we die. That is why we are so grateful to God for loving us enough to reveal this to us now, in this time of mercy and grace.

LXXIX
Examine Your Own Sin—But No One Else's

> Julian continues her discussion of sin, indicating that we are to constantly put our trust in God rather than ourselves. "By this understanding I am kept from arrogance and conceit," writes Julian, "while at the same time love's comfort and joy protect me from despair."
>
> At the end of the chapter, Julian touches on God's loneliness when we are exiled from the Divine that lives within ourselves. She will continue this thought in the following chapter.

This showing gave me yet more understanding: that when I become aware of sin, it is my own sin only, not another's. The Divine message that was given to me, however, is for all human beings, for all of us have separated ourselves from God. I am a member of the human race, and the happy comfort revealed to me is big enough for us all. I can examine my own life for sin and no other's—but I can share help and comfort with us all.

In this same showing I understood that I will again and again fall into sin, and so I learned to examine myself and question myself at all times. I do not know in what ways I will fall, nor can I predict how severely I will stumble. I only know I cannot trust myself not to sin. And yet our kind Protector revealed with great certainty and strength that Divine love is endless and unchangeable. By God's great goodness and grace, we are kept safe in our minds, and we shall never be separated from love. By this understanding I am kept from arrogance and conceit, while at the same time love's comfort and joy protect me from despair. This intimate showing came from our kind Protector, a lovely lesson of Divine comfort.

Through our sweetly intimate relationship with God, we will come to recognize that anything we see or feel, whether on the inside or the outside, that conflicts with this understanding is from the Enemy and not from God. That is why we should not trust any impulse that causes us to be careless with our lives and minds, for such carelessness is at odds with God's truth. We should reject such impulses, for they are in opposition to the Divine will.

If through our weakness or blindness we fall, then our kind Protector touches us and inspires us and calls us, so that we become aware of our brokenness. But God does not want us to dwell on this awareness; the Divine will would not have us become preoccupied with accusing ourselves or being exiled from ourselves. Instead, God wants us to quickly turn back to the Divine Presence. Until we hurry back to that Presence, God stands alone, watching us with sorrow. For we are God's joy and delight—and God is our medicine and our life.

(Of course when I say that God stands alone, I am not speaking of the happy company of Heaven, but of God's work here on Earth, as was revealed through this showing.)

LXXX
God Is Both Highest and Lowest

The word "worship," to which Julian refers both here and in earlier chapters, is another that had a quite different significance in the fourteenth century from what it does today. We think of worship as reverent praise offered to someone who is admired; it is a one-sided concept, an attitude that flows from the one who is inferior to the one who is superior. In Julian's day, however, the word was "worth-ship," similar to our concept of "worthiness," and it was a reciprocal thing: both participants in worship gained worth or value. In Old English, "worth" meant "a turning toward," "the process of making opposites equivalent," and "to come to be." This gives us a quite different notion from the one to which we are accustomed, one that is closer to Julian's meaning, though at first glance it may seem nonsensically radical: as we worship God, God worships us; our worth is increased, for we are transformed into God.

Julian's description of Christ standing "all alone" in the human mind may also seem contrary to what we have learned from Christian doctrine—and yet isn't this what Christianity has always taught: that Jesus Christ chose to take on himself the cost of human sin? Julian's revelation indicates a deeper meaning of this basic Christian tenet. Christ lives eternally in

> the human soul, insists Julian; he is tied to human nature by the very fact of his Being as well as ours. Ontologically, Jesus cannot be separated from the human identity—and it is he who bears within us the loneliness and anguish of sin, all the while keeping us forever safe.
>
> Repentance, then, is not motivated by guilt or fear (at least not from Julian's perspective), but by love for Jesus. We are drawn deeper into the spiritual life because of the love and longing that is also part of our very nature.

In this life, human beings grow toward God by three means, and by these same three, God is worshiped, while we are at the same time moved onward, kept, and saved. The first is by means of human intelligence and our innate powers of reason; the second is the Church's teachings; and the third is the inner work of the Holy Spirit's grace. These three come from a single God: God is the foundation of our human intelligence and of the Church, and God is the Holy Spirit. All these are separate gifts we should value individually, to which we should give our attention. For they work together in us continually; and God wants us to know the ABCs of these great things in this life, so that we can learn them in their entirety in Heaven, and be moved ever onward.

By faith we know that God alone took on our human nature, and no one else. And we know that Christ alone completed the work of our salvation, and no one else, and now He completes the end of it by dwelling with us here in this life, directing us and bringing us into friendship with God. And Christ will keep doing this so long as any soul is left on Earth who needs to be brought to Heaven—and if there were only one soul left on Earth, Christ would be with that person until He had brought her into friendship with Him. I believe what the priests teach us about angels' service to humanity, but I did not see any angels in the showings I received. For Christ is the One who is nearest and gentlest, highest and lowest, the One who does all. He not only does all that we need, but all that increases us and adds to our joy in Heaven.

Christ waits for us with sorrow and mourning, united with all that is true in our selves. He feels the brokenness and regret and pain we feel when we are not united with our Protector. Everything within our own minds that moves us forward is Christ living in us. Many of us are seldom aware that He is there, but He is always aware of us until He has brought us out from all our sighing and sorrow. When we fall into sin, taking our leave of Christ's mind within us, neglecting to keep our souls whole—then Christ keeps them whole by Himself, standing guard over us with sorrow and yearning.

Respect and kindness impels us to turn back quickly to our Protector, so that He is not left all alone for long. We are the only reason why He is here; He is here alone with us all. And when I put myself outside of Him because of my sin, despair, or laziness, then I leave my Protector standing alone in my mind. This is how it is with all of us who sin. But no matter how many times we do this, Christ's goodness never allows us to be all alone. His presence with us is permanent; with gentle tenderness, He takes away our guilt, always shielding us from any blame in His sight.

LXXXI
God Sees Our Lives as Penance

As the Apostle Paul wrote in 2 Corinthians 4:17, "Our light affliction, which is but for a moment, is working for us a far more exceeding and eternal weight of glory" (NKJV). It is the suffering of this life (the longing we feel for God, the blindness that separates us from awareness of the Divine Presence) that drives us toward God; it is the only penance God asks of us.

Our good Protector reveals the Divine Being in a variety of ways, both in Heaven and on Earth, but I saw God take no place as home except the human soul.

God revealed the Divine on Earth through the Incarnation and Christ's Endurance on the Cross. And God is seen on Earth in other ways, such as in the revelation where I saw God in a single Point. God is also seen in life's journeys; in other words, God is here with us, leading us, and God will never leave us as we wander like pilgrims on our way to Heaven's joy. God reigns over the Earth—but only in a human soul does God find a resting place. Your soul is the City of God, and God will never leave this most worthy throne.

Marvelous and solemn is the place where the Protector dwells, bringing all into Oneness. This is why God wants us to quickly respond whenever we feel the Divine touch, rejoicing more in the wholeness of God's love than we sorrow over our frequent failures. For of all our actions, God finds the most worth in lives lived with gladness and laughter, even in the midst of our penance. (From God's perspective, our entire lives are a penance; the constant longing we feel for God is our penance, a penance God both creates in our minds and helps us to bear.)

Divine love makes God long for us; Divine wisdom, truth, and straightforwardness make God allow us to be here on Earth, separated in some measure from God; and God puts in us this same mixture of longing for something more while we live in what we have here on Earth. This is our natural penance, and this is the best penance, the only penance we need, for it is a part of our minds and always will be until we are fulfilled at last, when we have the Gift for which we have always longed. This is why God wants us to set our minds on the Transcendent, that which goes beyond all other joys and exceeds all other glory. We are to turn our minds from the pain we feel here in this life to the joy we trust awaits us.

LXXXII
In Both Our Rising and Our Falling We Are Kept Whole in Love

> Yet again, Julian discusses the paradoxical dual reality we experience during mortal life: "As we look at God, we fall not; as we look at ourselves, we cannot keep from falling; and both these perspectives are real." She goes on to affirm, "The tension between these two realities is good for us."

Our considerate Protector now revealed the meaning of the soul's sadness and anxiety: "I know you would live for My love joyously and gladly, enduring all the discipline and repentance that comes to you—but since you live separated from God, your love for Me will cause you to suffer all the sorrow, troubles, and distress that come to you. This is reality. But since you are not to blame for the condition in which you find yourself, don't let yourself grieve over it too much."

From this I understood that the Protector looks at the servant with pity and not with blame. The reality of our temporal lives means that we sin; this is just the way life is on Earth. God loves us endlessly, while we sin habitually; God demonstrates only gentleness, though we sorrow and mourn, granting us discernment so that we turn to see Divine mercy, clinging to God's love and goodness. We realize then that God is our only medicine, while we can do nothing but fall from Divine perfection. In humility, we finally get past the sight of our sin, as we please God by faithfully understanding the everlasting Divine love, thanking and praising God.

God said to me, "I love you, and you love Me, and Our love for each other shall never be separated into two pieces. For your good, I endure all pain." I heard these words spoken to my spiritual being: "I keep you completely safe."

God yearns for us to live in this way—both longing for more while enjoying total fullness, as this lesson in love teaches us—and this Divine yearning showed me that anything that opposes our true selves comes not from God but from our souls' Enemy. God wants us to understand this as the grace-filled light of Divine intimacy and love reveals it. And if any of God's lovers on this Earth are ever kept from falling, I know nothing about it; God did not show me any such thing. Instead, I saw this: that in falling and rising we are always kept and treasured in the unity of love.

As we look at God, we fall not; as we look at ourselves, we cannot keep from falling; and both these perspectives are real. But the vision of our Protector God is the highest reality. Gratitude for this deepest reality ties us to God, and God reveals this deep truth hidden in all life. I understood that while we live on this Earth, we travel faster and more directly on our spiritual journeys if we can keep both perspectives in mind at once. The tension between these two realities is good for us: the higher, more spiritual perspective gives us comfort and deep Divine joy, while at the same time the lower, earthly perspective makes us anxious and often ashamed. Our good Protector wants us to focus on the higher viewpoint, even while we cannot escape the lower until the moment when we are brought up into Heaven. There our Protector Jesus will be our reward, and we will be filled with joy and delight that never ends.

LXXXIII
Life, Love, and Light

> Julian continues to analyze her revelations more deeply, finding the common threads that run through them all. Here she recognizes life, love, and light, and goes on to focus on light, implying that the light we experience is both Divine and a natural result of our human intellects, as well as our faith. In the next chapter, she will turn her focus to love.

Throughout all the revelations, I touched, saw, and felt three of the Divine qualities, and it was these sense perceptions that made the showings so strong and powerful. This was true of all the showings but especially the twelfth, where God spoke: "It is I." The three Divine qualities the revelations revealed are these: life, love, and light. Divine life gives to God an amazing familiarity and comfortable quality; Divine love is full of gentle consideration; and Divine light is the essence of reality's endless relationships. These properties are contained in a single sweet unity, a unity to which the human mind naturally clings with all its might, becoming one with it.

With deep awe and amazement at this understanding and the feeling it gave me of harmony and union, I realized that our minds (our intellectual abilities as well as the very substance of what makes us who we are) are built in God. They are the highest gifts we have received, grounded in our inherent natures, and yet they are also Divine.

Our faith is a natural light that indicates the coming of endless day, our Divine Parent: Father God, Mother Christ, and Protector Spirit, who lead us through our temporal lives. This light is carefully measured out to us, so that we have what we need to get through the night. This light gives us life, while the night is the cause of all our pain and sadness. God thanks us and rewards us for enduring the darkness. With mercy and grace, we hold firm, believing that our light is real, and that we can follow it with wisdom and strength.

And when all sadness ends, suddenly our eyes will open. In the clear daylight, our vision will be complete. In this way I came to understand that our faith gives light to our night, and that same light is God, our endless day—our Maker and our Rescuer, that which is God, Christ Jesus, and the Holy Spirit.

LXXXIV
Love

> As Julian focuses on love, she once again unites the strands she has separated: the light she discussed in the previous chapter (our human intellect as well as the essence of our being), she insists, is also love. With her medieval obsession with intellectual analysis, she then divides love into another three strands, but she ultimately affirms simply, "In the end, all shall be love."

The light is love, and God's wisdom measures it out to us exactly as we need it. The light is never so great that we see complete daylight, nor is it ever kept from us so that utter darkness falls. It is just enough light for us to live as we need, with hard work and pain, so that we earn God's endless affirmation, the value given by God to us. I saw this in the sixth showing, where God said, "Thank you for your service and your hard work." In this way, love keeps us safe in faith and hope, and hope leads us deeper in love. And in the end, all shall be love.

I understood this light—love—in three different ways. The first is love that was never created or made; the second is created love; and the third is love that is given. The love that was never created or made is God; created love is our soul in God; and the love that is given is virtue (goodness and strength for our souls). This is a sweet and functional gift, allowing us to love God as God . . . to love our own selves, who are in God . . . and to love all that God loves, on God's behalf.

LXXXV
All Is as It Is: All Is Well

> As Julian finally nears the end of her book, her words and thoughts exhausted, she yet again affirms one of her central themes: "All is well." God will never disappoint us.

As I saw these things, I was full of awe and amazement. Despite our shallow lives and our blindness, yet our courteous Protector always joyfully watches all this love at work in us. The best way to please God is by truly believing this, enjoying this vision along with God, in God. For as certainly as we shall live forever in God's delighted friendship, just so has God always known and loved us, since before time, and from the very beginning, we have been part of the Divine's endless purpose. In this love that has no beginning we were made, and in the same love we are kept safe and whole forever, so that our joy will never be lost. When the Last Day comes, and we are all brought up from this world, then we shall see in God all the secrets that are now hidden. And not one of us will want to say, "God, if only . . ." Instead, with one voice we shall say, "Be blessed, Protector God, for all is as it is, and all is completely well." And we will finally understand that everything is done just as it had been laid out before Creation.

LXXXVI
Love Was What It All Meant

> Having reached the end of her writing, may her book continue to live, and may her "showings" take root in our' minds and continue to grow, as Julian would have wished.
>
> Ultimately, Julian understands that all the theological inquiry and intellectual analysis is summed up into a single statement: love is God's only message to us. "Hold on to that love," concludes Julian, "and you will learn and understand more of the same love—but you will never learn nor understand anything else."

This book is begun by God's gift, by Divine grace, but I do not believe it has yet been finished. It is still developing and growing.

In love, we all pray, immersed in Divine action, thanking, trusting, enjoying. This is the prayer our good Protector wants from us; this is what I understood from the laughter in God's voice as I heard these words: "I am the source of all your longing, the foundation of all you ask." I understood from all this that our Protector wants our understanding to be deepened, and as we know more, we will receive more grace to love and cling to God. God looks at us—we who are God's heavenly treasure on Earth—with such great love, giving us more light and comfort, more heavenly delight, drawing our minds out of our sorrow and shadows into the Divine light.

After these showings, I kept wondering what they meant. What had our Protector been saying? I wanted to see more clearly. Finally, more than fifteen years later, I was given this spiritual message: "Do you really want to clearly see the Protector's meaning in the showings? Well, then, learn it well: Love was God's meaning. Who showed you these visions? Love. What were you shown? Love. Why were you shown these vision? For love. Hold on to that love, and you will learn and understand more of the same love—but you will never learn nor understand anything else."

And so I finally understood: Love was the meaning in everything God had shown me.

I saw completely and certainly that before we were ever made, we were loved. God's love for us has never diminished, and it never will. In this love, all Creation was made and continues to function; in this love, all things work out for our good; and in this love, we shall live forever. We began to exist when God created us—but Divine love for us has no beginning. Our beginnings sprang from that love.

And in love, we see God endlessly, world without end.

hazelnuts from Julian of Norwich

Meditations on Divine Love

by ELLYN SANNA

Paperback Price: $14.95

"The Spirit showed me a tiny thing, the size of a hazelnut," wrote the fourteenth-century mystic, Julian of Norwich. In Julian's vision, the fragile and insignificant hazelnut contains all of Creation—and yet it endures "because God loves it."

Seven hundred years before Rob Bell wrote Love Wins, Julian had already offered the world a vision of God's all-encompassing love. These prayer-poems, based on *All Shall Be Well: A Modern-Language Version of the Revelation of Julian Norwich*, are an accessible introduction to Julian's joyous theology of love.

Love Prayers
from Rumi & other Sufi Mystics

edited by DEVON HOLCOMBE

Paperback Price: $16.95

The Sufi mystics' religion was love–and God was their Beloved. Their relationship with the Beloved gave each moment meaning and joy.

As you pray with words inspired by Rumi and other Sufi mystics, you'll experience a new understanding of the Divine One who is everything and nothing, all that we can perceive and all that we cannot. You may even, like the Sufis, find yourself falling head over heels in love with a God who is present everywhere, within you and without. Whatever your religion (or lack of religion), these spiritual poems, inspired by ancient Sufism, will bring you into a deeper relationship with both the Divine and your true Self.

THE HEART OF MEDITATION
INTERFLOW:
THOUGHTS, PRAYERS, & MEDITATIONS

by GEORGE BREED

Paperback Price: $14.95

In this paperback collection of the e-book series titled *Meditations of the Heart*, the author offers bite-size entries into mindfulness and transformation. Each meditation could be used as a vehicle for greater consciousness—or as a prayer leading to deeper awareness of spiritual reality and being. One Amazon reviewer summarized: "Each tiny gem of a meditation holds meaning beyond and beneath the words, and each provides nourishment for the mind and the heart. Concise, simple, but packed with a powerful load of thought-provoking enlightenment, George Breed gives more to us in his meditations with a dozen or so words than most philosophers give in twelve dozen."

CELTIC NATURE PRAYERS
Prayers from an Ancient Well

by KENNETH MCINTOSH with LUCIE STONE

Paperback Price: $14.95

E-book Price: $5.99

Find God in Nature

Pray for Our Endangered Planet

Commune with God in nature using these ancient and modern prayers, compiled and written by Kenneth McIntosh, author of the bestselling *Water from an Ancient Well: Celtic Spirituality for Modern Life*. Just as the Celts found the Divine in every tree and blade of grass, so we too can be refreshed and enriched by a new connection with the Earth.

www.AnamcharaBooks.com

www.ingramcontent.com/pod-product-compliance
Lightning Source LLC
Chambersburg PA
CBHW060514080526
44586CB00012B/481